RIGHT TO EDUCATION

Anatomy of the Pennsylvania Case
and Its Implications for Exceptional Children

LEOPOLD LIPPMAN

I. IGNACY GOLDBERG

TEACHERS COLLEGE PRESS

Teachers College, Columbia University
New York and London

Foreword

Early in the body of this publication, in tracing the evolution of the social activism that resulted in the Pennsylvania case, the authors describe what they see as the characteristics of the mental retardation movement, by decades. A similar—indeed parallel—analysis may be offered with regard to the emerging role of special education:

In the 1950's, the field benefited from intensive involvement of the executive and legislative branches of government. Impetus came from the Federal level and quickly rippled out to most of the 50 states, as governors and their administrators followed the lead of President Kennedy in the 1960's.

Now, well into the 1970's, it appears that the *third* coordinate branch of government—the judiciary —is also assuming a major role through their encouraging advocacy on behalf of handicapped children. Even in the few months since the final court order (May 1972) in the Pennsylvania case, there have been numerous extensions of the principle: to children with diverse handicaps, to the mentally ill, to residential facilities as well as conventional educational systems, even to correctional institutions. All this the Federal and state courts have begun to affirm.

The new ally (the American judicial system, with its basic concepts of due process) must nevertheless be seen as *one more* member of the team, rather than as the substitute squad. As the authors say repeatedly, and as counsel for the plaintiffs in the Pennsylvania case insisted from the beginning, litigation was merely one more tool in the kit of those who would improve the lives of retarded children. Legislation, executive leadership, publicity political action, and community organization continue to be important channels.

The magnitude of the problem of education of the handicapped is hard to gauge with precision since, for example, many of the children are invisible just because they are not receiving the services they need. They may be inappropriately placed in regular classes; they may be in state institutions; or they may be at home, out of school, and officially unknown to the educational system.

Millions of children of school age in the United States are considered to be handicapped in some way—mentally, physically, emotionally, sensorily; estimates run from 10% to as high as 25%. A somewhat lower number, of course, would require special education services. The Bureau of Education for the Handicapped of the United States Office of Education, on the basis of figures supplied by state departments of education, estimated over seven million children of school age (5-19 years) to be handicapped, with over one-third (38%) receiving special education services in 1968–69. The percentage served varies by handicapping condition, but in no category is the volume of service nearly satisfactory; and these figures take no account of the *quality* of the educational programs.

In September 1972, the Department of Health, Education, and Welfare published illuminating statistics on the number of mentally retarded persons living in the public institutions of the 50 states. At the end of fiscal year 1970, according to the report, almost 190,000 such persons were confined in these residential settings; almost 50% of them were between five and twenty years of age. It is probably safe to say that a majority of the school-age children were not receiving regular, continuing special education services appropriate to their needs and capabilities. Since the average length of stay in a public institution has been a matter of decades, many of those who are now adults received little or no educational attention *even as children.* It can be concluded therefore that the bulk of the institutionalized mentally retarded persons represent a grossly underserved and in that sense disadvantaged group.

This publication is the product of genuine collaboration between the coauthors, and the story of the product is in part the history of a warm cooperative relationship extending over more than 15 years. It is also the unique result of the melding of two quite different yet closely related professional careers.

The two men met in 1956. Ignacy Goldberg was at that time educational consultant to the National Association for Retarded

Children. His principal task was to travel the country stirring up official public interest in the then unfamiliar and somewhat unaccepted idea of special education for all retarded children. Leopold Lippman was executive director of the Washington Association for Retarded Children, the host state unit for that year's national convention of the Association. He filled a major role in staffing and publicizing the convention.

During the ensuing decade and a half, the two men pursued separate careers in different aspects of mental retardation. Ignacy Goldberg became Professor of Education at Teachers College, Columbia University, simultaneously giving of his energies and abilities in many professional capacities to become president of the American Association on Mental Deficiency and, later, the secretary of the International Association for the Scientific Study of Mental Deficiency. Leo Lippman moved from the State of Washington to California, where he served as executive secretary of the Study Commission on Mental Retardation, the first state comprehensive mental retardation planning body to confront the task set by the President's Panel on Mental Retardation; he then became California's Coordinator of Mental Retardation Programs. When he returned to his native New York in 1968 as the City's Director of Services for the Mentally and Physically Handicapped, he and Professor Goldberg again accelerated their cooperative efforts on many matters of common concern.

In the summer and fall of 1971, their interests converged around what became known as the "landmark" Pennsylvania case. Ignacy Goldberg was enlisted among the four internationally recognized "expert witnesses" at a hearing in Federal court in Philadelphia. In his testimony, of which he modestly quotes a small excerpt in this publication, Professor Goldberg affirmed his professional conviction that every retarded child can indeed benefit from education. The experts' testimony was so persuasive that the Commonwealth of Pennsylvania approached the plaintiffs to convert the adversary proceeding into a consent agreement.

Mr. Lippman, meanwhile, having undertaken a study of different national value systems, which resulted in his publication, *Attitudes Toward the Handicapped: A Comparison Between Europe and the United States*, was intrigued with the dynamics of the social and political process that the Pennsylvania case represented.

Immediately recognizing the larger implications of the case for educators, for the legal profession, for social activists, and for families of all handicapped children, the authors together undertook an intensive investigation into the background, the mechanics, and the outcomes of the litigation. This publication is the product of that collaboration.

Professor Gunnar Dybwad, of Brandeis University, who was asked to review critically a portion of the manuscript in draft form, offered this comment: "It is a good paper, carefully researched, but of necessity selective—and that makes it your paper. There just is no way to cover it all—'all' just is not in the ken of anyone."

He is correct. Every creative effort is a work of art, and art involves selection. The decisions reflected in this account of the "Right to Education" case are the decisions of sensitive, perceptive, creative people, each coming from a different disciplinary background, but both generalists in the most complimentary sense of that term.

The monograph represents also the creative and intelligent effort of many individuals, as evident in the text. To each of them is expressed the appreciation and respect of both the authors and the editor. Without them, this report would not have been possible.

Although footnotes in the body of this volume are few in number, most of the source citations appear in the list of References at the end of the volume. It is anticipated that the serious student of "Right to Education" action will use this list as a working bibliography; it points to key publications in special education, in litigation, and in social action toward the attainment of rights of the handicapped.

Separately (Appendix A) is a list of all the court cases cited in the body of the narrative. These fall generally into two categories: precedent cases in civil rights as distinguished from educational rights, and currently relevant cases in special education in its various ramifications.

The significance of the Pennsylvania case is, in a sense, the theme of this publication. The significance of this report is seen in its potential contribution to the field of special education (1) for its thorough and painstaking research into the genesis, the origin of this milestone case; (2) for its factual description of the procedure (this is what the authors mean by their subtitle, "The Anatomy of the Pennsylvania Case"); and (3) for its insight in drawing implications for further development of programs for the handicapped.

What can special educators learn from this account? This report raises more questions than it answers, but the raising of suitable questions is itself a creative act and a contribution to learning. Among those questions are: (1) What of "zero rejection"? Can special education, in its present structure, take care of all children regardless of handicap? (2) What are the implications for preparation of educational personnel in colleges and universities? (3) How will funds be obtained for such an enterprise? (4) What are the respective roles for government and private enterprise in the partnership task of educating handicapped children? (5) What is the age span for the clientele of concern to special educators?

The content of these questions is not new. Early in 1971, Sidney P. Marland, Jr., United States Commissioner of Education, called for the development of a national goal to provide full educational opportunity for every handicapped child in this country by 1980. The Bureau of Education for the Handicapped in the United States Office of Education has been working for two years toward the definition and attainment of that goal.

And there are stirrings elsewhere. In an article published in the July 1972 issue of *Déficience Mentale/Mental Retardation*, the bilingual magazine of the Canadian Association for the Mentally Retarded, D.R. Cameron, professor of educational psychology at the University of Alberta, wrote of "educating the ineducable" as it is currently practiced in the United Kingdom. He writes of reaching out, particularly in England and Wales, to serve the children formerly labeled "severely subnormal." American educators can indeed, as Lippman and Goldberg have repeatedly said in other contexts, learn from our colleagues in other parts of the world.

But for the moment—the moment that began with filing the complaint in January 1971 and that reached a climax with handing down the Federal court order in May 1972—the world looks to the innovation of litigatory action as pioneered in Pennsylvania.

This is an unusual publication in that the Appendices form almost as large a corpus as the main narrative. The longest Appendix (D) is the full text of the court order in the Pennsylvania case. This is included *in extenso* because the decision of the Federal Court was so significant that it forms an integral part of the story, and because it spells out the fundamental issues confronted in the Pennsylvania case. To the motivated advocate for handicapped children, the Federal Court order is a working script for future action.

This is a timely publication; but it has been written, as have all publications in the Teachers College Series in Special Education, with the longer range in mind. In its implications for affirmative action, we believe it will be timely for many years to come.

Frances P. Connor
Chairman, Department of Special Education
Teachers College, Columbia University

Contents

CHAPTER 1

Introduction

The evolution of man as a social being is marked by increasing concern for the rights of his fellows. Look back just a few hundred years:

1215: No free man shall be taken or imprisoned or exiled or in any way destroyed . . . except by the lawful judgment of his peers or by the laws of the land.—*Magna Carta.*

1789: *Les hommes naissent et demeurent libres et égaux en droits.—Déclaration des Droits de l'Homme, Article Premier.*

1791: No person shall . . . be deprived of life, liberty, or property, without due process of law.—Constitution of the United States, Amendment V.

1868: No State shall make or enforce any law which shall abridge the privileges or immunities of citizens of the United States; nor shall any State deprive any person of life, liberty or property without due process of law, nor deny to any person within its jurisdiction the equal protection of the laws.—Constitution of the United States, Amendment XIV.

1954: In these days, it is doubtful that any child may reasonably be expected to succeed in life if he is denied the opportunity of an education. Such an opportunity, where the state has undertaken to provide it, is a right which must be made available to all on equal terms.—Supreme Court of the United States, in *Brown v. Board of Education.*

1971: The mentally retarded person has a right to proper medical care and physical therapy and to such education, training, rehabilitation and guidance as will enable him to develop his ability and maximum potential.—United Nations General Assembly.[1]

[1]See Appendix C for full text.

1

1972: It is ordered. . . . that the Commonwealth of Pennsylvania . . . provide, as soon as possible but in no event later than September 1, 1972, to every retarded person between the ages of six and twenty-one years as of the date of this Order and thereafter, access to a free public program of education and training appropriate to his learning capacities.—United States District Court, in *Pennsylvania Association for Retarded Children, Nancy Beth Bowman et al., v. Commonwealth of Pennsylvania, David H. Kurtzman et al.*[2]

There have been many ringing declarations of principle over the recent decades and indeed over the centuries. The foregoing quotes have been culled only from official public documents. Of them all, the ones dated 1868, 1954, and 1972 are perhaps the most important for the ultimate protection of the rights of handicapped persons.

In the short time since its promulgation, the Pennsylvania decision has already had substantial impact nationwide. Further effects may be anticipated. The Pennsylvania "Right to Education" case is a crucial part—but still only a part—of the movement toward equality of opportunity for all handicapped children and adults.

The Issues

Attitudes, expectations, even values are in a state of rapid change in the United States today. What was long taken for granted is now questioned and challenged. The "accepted ways" of dealing with social problems are no longer accepted. People are asserting their rights—as women, as students, as members of ethnic minorities, as behavioral deviants. Those who cannot speak for themselves, such as children and the mentally retarded, have attracted spokesmen. A partnership of advocacy is taking form; and among the participants are parents of the handicapped, educators and other professional workers, and the new phenomenon of public-interest lawyers.

Furthermore, the partners are operating in a new arena: the courts. Litigation is not a substitute for all previous forms of social action; it is, rather, a major addition to the armamentarium of those who would obtain more effective services for the handicapped.

In a working paper prepared for the 1960 White House Conference on Children and Youth, Gunnar Dybwad, then executive director of the National Association for Retarded Children, called attention to the denial of diagnostic, educational, and other services to mentally retarded persons and commented: "Insufficient attention has been given in the past to the legal status of the mentally retarded child and adult, particularly with reference to the degree of legal

[2]The court opinion, order, and injunction contained numerous other provisions of major importance. See Appendix D.

protection required as related to the degree of the mental handicap" (Dybwad, 1964, p. 210).

The Task Force on Law of the President's Panel on Mental Retardation (1963, p. 20) laid down the broad principle: "Our basic position is that all rights normally held by anyone are also held by the retarded." The statement could have been, and now should be, extended to all exceptional, handicapped, or disadvantaged persons—indeed, to all the deviant and dependent members of society. The denial of rights is most grievous in childhood, because those are the formative years; deprivation in the first two decades of life has a blighting effect on the individual forevermore.

The challenge has been concisely expressed: "Equal Justice for the Unequal" (Allen, 1969a). Discrimination exists. Often it is unwitting, but the impact is none the less. The child from a non-English-speaking family, or from a different cultural background, will perform less well on "intelligence tests." The orthopedically disabled child must constantly cope with architectural barriers in the school, the recreation centers, and wherever else he goes for service programs. The youngsters with visual, aural, or neurological disabilities usually must accommodate to the setting in which they find themselves, rather than the other way around.

The issue is whether the individual has a *right* to be deviant (Segal, 1972). The professional field of special education affirms that he has that right, and that it is society's—and specifically the school's—obligation to accommodate to the child. The relevant concept is "zero rejection" (Lilly, 1970: Goldberg, 1971).

Related to the basic issue are many specific questions, including:

—What is the responsibility of the public school system to educate exceptional children? What of children in state residential facilities? What is the role of the private schools? What of handicapped persons beyond the customary school-age years? Whose responsibility is it to pay for special education under each of these circumstances?

—What is the best way to provide for the developmental and educational needs of handicapped children? How is this criterion different from "what is best for all children"? (Aside from the effect on the exceptional child, what is the impact of segregated education on the "normal" child?)

—Are there circumstances in which it is appropriate to provide for handicapped children a *type* of education that is different from that provided for "normal" children? Should the handicapped have a different *quality* of education, with differently qualified *teachers*?

—Should special education of retarded children start at a later age, and end at an earlier age, than education of other children? Are children who are blind, deaf, physically or neurologically disabled, better served, during their early years, in totally specialized facilities designed to help overcome their disabilities? At what stage, if ever, should they be incorporated into the main stream of education and of society generally? Should the school *day* be shorter? What is the role of preschool programs?

—Does educational labeling impose stigma on the child? Is the effect lifelong? What are the countervailing considerations, as between appropriately specialized educational services and the segregation that may result?

This publication details the anatomy of the Pennsylvania "Right to Education" case, which was filed in Federal District Court January 7, 1971, and on which the final Court Opinion, Order, and Injunction was issued May 5, 1972. There was more to the case than a decision binding upon the Commonwealth of Pennsylvania, its Department of Education and Department of Public Welfare, and the local and intermediate school districts of the Eastern District of Pennsylvania. Even before the final opinion and order were handed down, there were ripples of effect within the state, and growing impacts elsewhere. In the District of Columbia, in Alabama, and in other jurisdictions, Federal judges issued opinions, orders, and injunctions consistent with the Pennsylvania decision; parents of the handicapped and concerned professionals in many other states looked closely and imaginatively at their own programs in the light of the court ruling; and young, rights-oriented lawyers became aware of a new subject area for positive litigatory action.

Beyond the specifics of the particular case, therefore, this publication explores the implications of the Pennsylvania decision on the right to education of retarded children. It looks beyond the children to adults, beyond the retarded to all the handicapped, beyond education to treatment and habilitation. There are seeds, in the Pennsylvania case, for imaginative and creative action by educators (teachers, administrators, and trainers of teachers), by other professionals concerned with handicapped children and adults, by rights lawyers, and of course by parents of the handicapped, working with their own organizations.

The essence of the Pennsylvania case is the affirmation of the right of all children to equal access to educational opportunity. The implementation of this principle may well occupy the parents and professional friends of exceptional children for the next decade.

CHAPTER 2

History and Evolution of the Concept

The concept of equal access to educational opportunity for handicapped children began in modest (one might say unrecognizable) ways in the mid-nineteenth century. The early state institutions for the "feeble-minded" in the United States, drawing on the experimental work of Itard and Seguin in Europe, were intended and planned as educational and habilitative resources. Similarly, blind children and deaf children were offered specialized training in residential facilities (Goldberg, 1952, pp. 24–27; Wallin, 1924, pp. 37–39).

The first efforts at special educational services *within the community*, however, came early in the twentieth century, with the assignment of teachers to special classes. Providence offered special classes for the retarded in 1895, and Springfield, Boston, and Chicago also started them before the turn of the century, with Philadelphia and Los Angeles coming soon after (Doll, 1962, pp. 39–40). The earliest classes were typically for the mildly retarded, now called "educable." The New York City Board of Education, in the first decade of this century, established "ungraded" classes, later known as classes for "children with retarded mental development" (CRMD), a designation still in existence.

State legislation, at the outset permissive, in many cases later mandatory, gave additional impetus to special education at the local school district level. New Jersey, in 1911, was the first state to legislate special education, first for the mildly retarded ("educable") and later for the more severely retarded ("trainable").[1] By 1927 a number of states had followed New Jersey's lead, and by the early 1950's first California and then other states were beginning to mandate special educational services for the mentally retarded (Wallin, 1966, pp. 118–123).

It is significant, in historical perspective, to note that the development of special classes for the mentally retarded in the public schools, first on a local basis and gradually through state legislative authorization and mandate, had the effect of changing the concept of the state institution from educational to custodial. The pioneering Seguin, in his classic *Idiocy: and Its Treatment by the Physiological Method* (1866), had written:

> The establishments founded for idiots have been called by various names—Schools, Institutions, Asylums, etc. . . . We are aware that the appellation of asylum has been attached to several of the most important schools. But this term conveys exclusively the idea of a custodian, lifelong place of retreat, whereas the institution or school is only temporarily open for educational and physiological treatment. In it idiots and their congeners are expected to remain during the period assigned by nature for progress in young persons, unless it sooner becomes manifest that they cannot be improved at all or any more, in which case their parents should take them out to make room for new pupils.

In 1961, the Board of Education of the State of Washington gave new scope to the established terminology. The State Legislature that year had attempted to put restraints on the expenditure of funds for education in the state residential facilities for the mentally retarded, by specifying that funds appropriated to the State Superintendent of Public Instruction might be spent for handicapped pupils in state institutions only for "children who meet the criteria of educability to be established by the State Board of Education." The State Board responded to the challenge by formulating the following definition of educability:

> A child shall be deemed educable if he possesses the potential to respond to and benefit from educational experiences in terms of such factors as social competence, emotional stability, self-care, a degree of vocational competency or intellectual growth.

This definition was interpreted by parents, by superintendents of state residential facilities for the retarded, and by the State

---

[1]The descriptive terminology originated by educators for their professional convenience later became encoded in the statutes by action of state legislatures, and often assumed the status of objective and discrete categories. Such rigid classifications, as with the original label of "mentally retarded," have a cumulatively stigmatizing effect. See Goldberg, 1971; Goffman, 1963; also "Combating Stigma Resulting from Deformity and Disease," Leonard Wood Memorial, New York, 1969, and Edgerton, Robert B., *The Cloak of Competence*, University of California Press, 1967.

Superintendent of Public Instruction, as embracing all children. Never—at least until the interim orders of the Federal Courts in Pennsylvania and Alabama in 1971—was so sweeping a provision given the force of official mandate.

A "Declaration of General and Special Rights of the Mentally Retarded" was adopted in 1968 by the International League of Societies for the Mentally Handicapped. This document, although it did not have the force of law, gave international recognition to the concept of "rights," and it set a standard for positive thinking about mentally retarded persons. In the context of special education, the relevant statements were:

Article I—The mentally retarded person has the same basic rights as other citizens of the same country and same age.

Article II—The mentally retarded person has a right to proper medical care and physical restoration and to such education, training, habilitation and guidance as will enable him to develop his ability and potential to the fullest possible extent, no matter how severe his degree of disability. No mentally handicapped person should be deprived of such services by reason of the costs involved.

Similar language was later embodied in a resolution adopted by the United Nations General Assembly (see Appendix C).

The organization of professional workers in special education, the Council for Exceptional Children, at its 1971 convention adopted a policy statement that asserted and spelled out "Basic Commitments and Responsibilities to Exceptional Children" (text reproduced in Appendix B). The opening paragraphs laid out the concept:

Education is the right of all children.

The principle of education for all is based on the philosophical premise of democracy that every person is valuable in his own right and should be afforded equal opportunities to develop his full potential. . . .

Because of their exceptionality, many of the children need to begin their school experiences at earlier ages than are customary for children in our society, many need formal educational services well into adulthood, and many require health and social services that are closely coordinated with school programs.

The policy statement then elaborated the major topics: the goal and commitment of special education; implementation of universal education, including compulsory services and compulsory attendance; special education within the schools; the relations of special and regular school programs; the need for flexibility; and government responsibility for support of special education.

It was in 1970, in California, that retarded children first had their day in court. Actually, some of the children had been *called* retarded and proved not to be; but the right to appropriate evaluation and educational services that was enunciated in this case proved to benefit the truly mentally retarded as well as those who had been mislabeled. The case was *Diana v. State Board of Education.*

The previous year, the Mexican-American Education Research Project of the California State Department of Education had examined the testing and school placement of children of Mexican descent in classes for the "educable mentally retarded." It was found that children whose native or family language was Spanish, and whose cultural environment was different from the normative Anglo society of California, had been placed in classes for the mentally retarded on the basis of conventional psychological tests. When they were retested a year later, however, in a specially modified Spanish-language version of the Wechsler Intelligence Scale for Children, many of them scored significantly higher, and some moved out of the range labeled "retarded" (Chandler and Plakos, 1969). The report concluded: "The results of this investigation indicate that many Mexican-American pupils may have been placed in EMR classes solely on the basis of performance on an invalid IQ test," and it offered the following recommendations:

School district personnel should review the cases of Spanish surnamed pupils currently enrolled in EMR classes; those pupils who appear to have difficulty in using the English language because Spanish is their native language should be retested with the Spanish version of the WISC.

Special personnel should be enlisted to assist the school psychologist in testing pupils who have a language barrier.

A formal request should be made of the testing corporation to make certain changes in the Spanish version of the WISC.

A "transition" program should be provided for pupils who need special instruction in the use of the English language. Such a program might include English-as-a-second-language (ESL) instruction and bilingual instruction in the basic subjects.

Long-range plans should be made to improve the present methods and instruments used for assessing pupils prior to referral to EMR classes, particularly those pupils with a cultural and linguistic background different from most of the English-speaking pupils.

Then came *Diana.* On behalf of nine Mexican-American children, a suit was filed in January 1970 in the Federal District Court for Northern California. The children ranged in age from 8 to 13 and in IQ score from 30 to 72. They had been assigned to classes for the mentally retarded in Monterey County. The suit charged that the placements were based on prejudicial testing procedures because the tests required facility in the English language, the questions were culturally biased, and the tests were standardized on white, native-born Americans (President's Committee on Mental Retardation, 1971a, pp. 59–60). Noting that children of Spanish surname constituted a significant proportion of the student population in Monterey County, but a far larger percentage of the children in EMR classes, the plaintiffs brought a "class action" to protect all Mexican-American children against inappropriate testing and placement. An agreement was signed by the contesting parties, as a resolution of the court case, in which it was stipulated: (1) Children are to be tested in their primary language. Interpreters may be used when a bilingual examiner is not available. (2) Mexican-American and Chinese children (another significant foreign-speaking minority in California) who have been placed in EMR classes are to be retested and evaluated. (3) Special efforts are to be extended to aid misplaced children to readjust to regular classroom placements. (4) The State of California will undertake immediate efforts to develop and standardize an appropriate IQ test.[2]

---

[2]*Diana v. State Board of Education* and several other cases on related issues are summarized in Weintraub, Frederick J., "Recent Influences of Law on the Identity and Placement of Children in Programs for the Mentally Retarded," in PCMR, 1971a, pp. 51–75. The treatment of Spanish-speaking children in the schools of California quickly gained wide attention. See, for example, "Language Gap: Where IQ Tests Can Fail," *San Francisco Examiner,* January 24, 1970; "San Diego Accused of Classing Ghetto Youths as Retarded," *Los Angeles Times,* April 26, 1970; "Language Bias in Calif. Schools Hit," *Washington Post,* May 27, 1970; "Mexican-American Hostility Deepens in Tense East Los Angeles," *New York Times,* September 4, 1970.

CHAPTER 3

Background and Roots of the Pennsylvania Case

Mental retardation—and societies' attempts to cope with it—goes back millennia. Three decades, however, encompass the modern era, and each has its own distinctive attributes and emphases.

The 1950's were the years of parent organization, of public awareness, of demonstration programs, and of legislative action.

There had been local organizations of parents of retarded children (and of citizens interested in other handicapping conditions) in the 1940's and earlier, but the founding convention of the National Association for Retarded Children in October 1950 truly marked the beginning of a new era.[1] The establishment of NARC stimulated local and state organization efforts of parents of the mentally retarded; it helped parents find each other and begin to replace their feelings of guilt with mutual emotional support; and it led to an extensive program of public information and sensitization, which brought the subject of mental retardation into the open (Katz, 1961; Segal, 1970).

As the local and state associations for retarded children (and adults) gained strength, they began to make an impact on school boards, state legislatures, and other public bodies. They also began communication with voluntary agencies in the fields of health and social service. The most important activity of the 1950's, however, was the spate of new service programs established by the associations themselves. These served two purposes: they began to

[1]The national organization of United Cerebral Palsy Associations was founded only months before NARC, in 1949.

10

meet the needs of retarded children and adults, and they served as demonstration models for public and voluntary community service agencies (Lippman, 1970).

In the mid-1950's there were also major developments at the national legislative level. Senator Lister Hill (Alabama) and Congressman John E. Fogarty (Rhode Island) introduced and steered to enactment highly important legislation, both substantive and budgetary. The hearings and other public informational activities undertaken by Senator Hill and by Congressman Fogarty were of value secondary only to the legislation itself, in that they brought about an increased awareness and acceptance of mental retardation and other handicapping conditions.

The 1960's were years of executive leadership at the national level, of comprehensive mental retardation planning at the state level, and of discovery of new concepts of service in Europe.

The inauguration of John F. Kennedy as President of the United States launched another phase of public concern for the mentally retarded. The appointment of the President's Panel on Mental Retardation in October 1961 and the submission of its report a year later posed the subject as a matter of national importance and one on which the Federal Government had an obligation to provide and to stimulate service.

An outgrowth of the work of the President's Panel was another development that assumed major importance in its own right. This was the preparation, by each of 53 states and jurisdictions, of a comprehensive mental retardation plan. Thousands of public officials and private citizens looked at the existing patterns of services in their states, studied the needs of retarded persons and their families, and developed recommendations to bring into existence the "continuum of service" that the President's Panel had proposed. The implementation of those state plans is still under way (Lippman, 1970).

Travelers to Europe, including several Missions sent by the President's Panel on Mental Retardation, as well as individual parents, educators, architects, and others, brought back word that in some countries (notably Scandinavia and The Netherlands) programs for the mentally retarded were far more enlightened, humane, and habilitative than in the United States (Kugel and Wolfensberger, 1969; Lippman, 1972). Such reports stirred people in the various states to review what they were doing and to consider alternative approaches.

The 1970's appear to be the era of litigation, of "landmark" court decisions, and of social action.

As the voluntary sector, the legislatures, and the executive branch of government each in its turn had an important part in the development of appropriate services for the mentally retarded, the turn has now come for the judiciary. This is not to say that judges are replacing legislators or governors as change agents, but rather that a new group of actors and a new scene of action have become involved.

Through the courts, starting with California in 1970, Pennsylvania and Alabama in 1971–72, and others proliferating rapidly, there is coming a new assertion of the rights of handicapped persons. The "right to education" case in Pennsylvania was quickly followed by "right to treatment," "right to habilitation," and other claims advanced by plaintiffs, often accepted by defendants and confirmed by the courts.

Litigation, then, added to existing statutes and potential legislative action, and supported by commitments from the executive branch and administrative agencies, sets the framework for a decade of positive social action. To the judiciary and members of the bar, past decisions of the courts are useful precedents; to parents, educators, and other advocates of the rights of the handicapped, the court decisions form one more group of levers with which to move society toward more equitable treatment of the handicapped.

The Precedent Case

The groundwork for the outcome of the Pennsylvania "Right to Education" case was laid more than 17 years earlier, when the Supreme Court of the United States, in *Brown v. Board of Education*, overturned earlier decisions upholding "separate but equal" educational facilities for children of different races. The unanimous 1954 decision affirmed:

[Education] is required in the performance of our most basic responsibilities. . . . It is the very foundation of good citizenship. It is a principal instrument for awakening the child to cultural values, in preparing him for later . . . training, and in helping him to adjust normally to his environment. It is doubtful that any child may reasonably be expected to succeed in life if he is denied the opportunity of an education. . . .

Today, education is perhaps the most important function of the state and local governments. . . . Where the state has undertaken to provide it, [it] is a right which must be available to all on equal terms.

Soon after the decision was handed down, a letter to the editor of *Children Limited*, bi-monthly newspaper of the National Association for Retarded Children, quoted the essential paragraph and commented: "You will recognize, I am sure, that this statement of equal opportunity applies to the handicapped as it does to the minorities."[2] The editor may have recognized the applicability, but no one moved for judicial affirmation until another 16 years had passed.

It is noteworthy, however (and the attorney for the plaintiffs in the 1971 Pennsylvania case noted it in his memorandum to the court), that John W. Davis, the attorney for South Carolina in the 1954 *Brown v. Board of Education* case, had opened his argument to the Supreme Court:

> May it please the Court, I think if the appellants' construction of the Fourteenth Amendment should prevail here, there is no doubt in my mind that it would catch the Indian within its grasp just as much as the Negro. If it should prevail, I am unable to see why a state would have any further right to segregate its pupils on the ground of sex or on the ground of age or *on the ground of mental capacity.* (Emphasis added.)

Counsel for South Carolina was right, of course; and it was on this premise that the Pennsylvania Association for Retarded Children *et al.* brought their case before the United States District Court for the Eastern District of Pennsylvania in January 1971.

Extension of the Principle

Viewed as social history, the decade of the 1960's appears as the time when oppressed minorities in the United States began to assert their rights. The dominant and most widely recognized movement was civil rights (Berger, 1967). Blacks, Chicanos, American Indians, and other ethnic groups began to speak up, to demonstrate, to demand, to fight, and occasionally to sue for the rights they considered their due. The action ranged from sit-ins at Southern lunch counters to violent revolt in Watts and Newark; and by the turn of the decade blacks in the South and the North, Chicanos in the Southwest, Puerto Ricans in the Northeast, and other ethnic minorities began to find doors of opportunity opening in employment, in housing, in places of public accommodation.

Not only ethnic minorities but other previously ignored subgroups likewise began to assert their rights. Throughout the country, but especially in the major urban centers, the impoverished recipients of public assistance organized the National Welfare Rights Organization. Consisting mainly of women recipients of Aid to Families with Dependent Children, NWRO used every technique the civil-rights activists had developed, and more: demonstrations,

[2]*Children Limited,* June 1955, p. 9.

sit-ins, takeovers of social work conferences, petitions, meetings with Congressmen, caravans to state capitals, insistence on legislative and administrative changes—and litigation.

Tenants, homosexuals, and women were among the other oppressed subgroups of the American population who began to express their convictions that they too were entitled to respect and to equal treatment.

The "war on poverty," which began as an innovation of the national administration in the early 1960's, led, among its less-anticipated results, to the encouragement of young, idealistic attorneys to enter the new field of "poverty law." The more familiar work of the public defenders, the Legal Aid Societies, and the American Civil Liberties Union—all of whom had represented unpopular and generally impecunious clients—was now augmented by the "rights lawyers," who were often financed by Federal funds, with the express authority to bring suit in behalf of their clients, even against a State or Federal Government itself.

The Harvard Center for Law and Education publishes an unusual periodical, *Inequality in Education*, which deals with mistreatment or discrimination against various categories of children. In a group of articles headed "Special Miseducation," (Hall, 1970, p. 20), the principle of "rights" with respect to education of exceptional children was formulated in these terms:

As they have done in Boston, poverty lawyers located elsewhere can beat their writs into community organizers as a technique for remedying some of the system's worst abuses. But there are many other, more traditional, legal avenues open and the situation is appalling enough to demand that they be explored.

First and most common to large urban areas is the case of children who would be eligible for state-mandated special programs but who are receiving no services because of inadequate space, inadequate screening programs, or insufficient funds. Where state statutes and regulations spell out criteria for these which local boards must follow but simply do not, a suit requiring conformity between practice and requirement should be helpful and fairly straightforward.

But if the language of the enabling legislation is permissive and the local district is only encouraged to maintain special programs, the individual student no longer has a statutory right to differential treatment.

Enter the state and federal constitutions. The former usually require the provision of a universal free education explicitly. And though the latter makes no reference to a right to an education, many recent commentators have made convincing cases for the idea that it is implicitly there. Under either document, anyone attempting to establish a non-statutory constitutional claim on some kind of differential school treatment must elevate the asserted but as yet unaccepted right to an education up to a right to a special education.

That would be no mean feat. But if a court accepted the argument, a series of ancillary (and entirely worthwhile) duties would fall to the local systems including: adequate universal access to the kind of tests which could identify legitimate special needs; adequate re-test provisions to check on placements; and services based not on the special classification but special need.

CHAPTER 4

Development of the Pennsylvania Case

What eventually became a national bellwether case on the issue of education started with concern for the mentally retarded residents of Pennhurst State School and Hospital. Pennhurst, located in Chester County, Pennsylvania, was a state residential facility for retarded persons. It had a rated bed capacity, according to the American Association on Mental Deficiency Directory of Residential Facilities for the Mentally Retarded (1968), of 2,126 and a resident population of 3,013. It was one of nine state residential facilities under the administrative responsibility of the Pennsylvania State Department of Public Welfare. It was neither the oldest nor the newest, but it was within a few residents of being the largest, and it had the worst reputation among parents and the public. Half the Pennhurst residents were over age 30, and three-fourths of them had been classified as profoundly or severely retarded. By far the largest number of residents lived in rooms with 30 or more other retarded persons.

Around the United States there had been other state institutions for the mentally retarded where conditions ranged from poor to abominable. This was, indeed, the norm rather than the exception. In the "best" and most affluent states, as well as the poorest and most backward, conditions were often wretched and dehumanizing. Physical plants were poorly designed, massively large, and grossly overcrowded; staff personnel were inadequately trained, often underpaid, and numerically inadequate for the number of handicapped persons in their charge; residents remained in idleness and deteriorated, rather than receiving habilitative services and progressing. The pattern of restraint and simple custody described for Renaissance Europe by Foucault (1971) and for nineteenth-century America by Rothman (1971) prevailed in the public institutions for the mentally retarded in the last third of the twentieth century. It was not deliberate cruelty (although there were cases of abuse and sadism) but rather arrant neglect. The optimism with which Seguin and other pioneers had launched residential programs for the feeble-minded a century earlier had been replaced by an atmosphere of hopelessness in which the line-level staff and many of the professional and administrative personnel were mere agents of a neglectful and uncaring society. One writer described several public facilities as "Christmas in Purgatory" (Blatt and Kaplan, 1966), and parents of retarded persons in many states across the land believed that the pictured institutions (not identified in the book) were the ones where their children lived.

Nevertheless, if Pennhurst was not the worst (and many people said it was), it was monstrously bad. In 1972, L. Steuart Brown, by then chairman of the Northeast Regional Legal Action Committee of the National Association for Retarded Children, characterized it as "a Dachau, without ovens." Brown, an engineer by profession and an active and long-time volunteer leader in the Pennsylvania Association for Retarded Children and its Montgomery County Chapter, described the scene at Pennhurst in these terms:

Large numbers of retarded persons have been herded together to live as animals in a barn, complete with stench. Many are forced into slave labor conditions; deprived of privacy, affection, morality; suffering the indignities of nakedness, beatings, sexual assaults and exposure. Some are doped out of reality with chemical restraints while others are physically deformed by the mechanical ones. Many are sitting aimlessly without motivations, incentives, hopes or programs.

There were investigations, newspaper reports, visits by legislators. All that resulted was a Senatorial report—no action.

At its annual convention in May 1969, the Pennsylvania Association for Retarded Children responded to the agonized distress of its members, and of other parents of the retarded through the state. After extended discussion—and recognizing that neither legislative approaches nor efforts to stimulate the executive branch had been effective—PARC authorized its president, James R. Wilson, Jr., to seek out and retain legal counsel. The attorney was to analyze the problem of Pennhurst in all its implications and to recommend an appropriate course of legal action.

Wilson and other leaders of the Pennsylvania Association had observed the growing attention on the national level to the rights of all persons, the social focus of the 1960's having been on members of racial minorities. They had noted a rising pattern of institutional change. Finally, they shared in the PARC membership's feeling of frustration. All of these perceptions were reflected in Wilson's presidential address to the 1969 convention, in which he asked (and answered):

What should PARC's role be in the years ahead? First, we should not simply reflect the changes which are taking place about us. We should initiate change, act as an agent of change. PARC's role in the past was based on yesterday's limited opportunities. However, the potential today is so very much greater, and so too are the opportunities. For instance, much of the recent social legislation has thrown the challenge back to us. Very simply, we have a hunting license to innovate. It's up to us!

The formal action that triggered what became the Pennsylvania "Right to Education" case was the adoption of the following resolution:

WHEREAS, the Pennsylvania Association for Retarded Children Chapters of five counties of Bucks, Chester, Delaware, Montgomery and Philadelphia served by Pennhurst met on April 29, 1969, to protest lack of improvement and continuing administrative malfeasance, misfeasance and/or nonfeasance at that institution; and

WHEREAS, the evidence and information collected by the Pennsylvania Association for Retarded Children Residential Care Committee confirms the inadequacy of Department of Public Welfare's efforts to improve or even arrest continued deterioration of that institution; and

WHEREAS, the residents of that institution continue to be abused, dehumanized and exposed to dangerous institutional practices; now, therefore, be it

RESOLVED that the Pennsylvania Association for Retarded Children, as the state-wide volunteer citizen association responsible to protect and promote the welfare of all mentally retarded Commonwealth citizens whether they be institutionalized or not, shall at this 19th Annual Convention authorize immediate retention of counsel by the Association for the filing of such legal action against the Department of Public Welfare as is necessary to either have it close Pennhurst or show just cause for its continuance; and be it further

RESOLVED that said counsel shall immediately define for the Association the feasibility of suit, the type of legal action and the most appropriate timing to be followed in view of current legislative efforts to investigate the existence of substandard state properties and instances of fiscal and administrative mismanagement of state properties. Once counsel's opinion and recommendations are available, the Executive Committee shall decide on action to take; and be it further

RESOLVED   that the President appoint two members of the Executive Committee to study and recommend to the President ways and means of funding the intent of this Resolution.

The language was broad enough to encompass whatever the attorney should recommend, subject to approval by the Legal Action Committee and the Executive Committee of PARC. As Wilson later expressed it: "We had gone the route of the executive and the bureaucracy to no avail. Now we decided to go the court route. We had reached the point where we believed that PARC should take a militant stance, vis-à-vis the state."

At the same convention, PARC adopted "A Bill of Rights for Pennsylvania's Retarded Citizens," whose opening paragraph declared:

Every retarded person, no matter how handicapped he is, is first of all in possession of human, legal and social rights. As much as possible, retarded persons, whether institutionalized or not, should be treated like other ordinary persons of their age are treated in the community. Every effort should be made to "normalize" the retarded person, to emphasize his similarity to normal persons and to diminish his deviant aspects.

Meanwhile—indeed within a few months in the same year—the Pennsylvania Federation Council for Exceptional Children was holding its tenth annual convention and the keynote address, "A Position Paper for Special Education in Pennsylvania—1969," was presented by the director of special education of the State Department of Education. His opening sentence was: "Pennsylvania has traditionally demonstrated national leadership as it goes about making provisions for the education of its children."

The keynoter spoke of a system of higher education preparing highly competent professional personnel; the application of instructional methods and techniques of the highest order; the introduction of new materials, equipment, and other instructional media; the modernization of schools to reflect a concern for quality education; the enactment of "landmark" legislation. Pennsylvania was also distinctive and ahead of other states in special education, he said, but he observed that a major concern of the special educator is his dilemma of how to make the transition from a static diagnostic model to a dynamic special education model.

The word "landmark" was to be used again, in quite a different context, two years later, when a Federal Court issued an order that would drastically change the provision of special education services for the handicapped children of Pennsylvania.

Counsel's Analysis and Recommendation

PARC President James Wilson and Residential Services Committee Chairman Dennis Haggerty acted quickly on the instructions of the resolution by retaining counsel to analyze the alternative courses open to deal with the Pennhurst problem and its ramifications. The man they found was Thomas K. Gilhool, a poverty lawyer then associated with a law firm in Philadelphia. He had recently participated in the successful prosecution of a number of "public interest" legal cases, dealing with such issues as welfare rights, public housing, and civil rights.

In a nine-page report to the PARC board in November 1969, Gilhool observed: "Litigation is one mode, among many, whereby the Association may encourage and expedite the kind of change it seeks in the care and treatment of retarded citizens." This, he said, was the concept underlying the action of the PARC convention resolution, and he endorsed it fully. He added, however:

There is nothing peculiar or extraordinary about litigation as a mode of social change. It is of the same cut as the other efforts of the Association to make use of other forums to define certain issues and to secure appropriate decisions by public officials.

Litigation has, inevitably, not only the function of securing a particular result, but of displaying facts and conditions clearly and precisely both before the public and before decision makers, of redefining the questions which must be answered by both. There is and should be considerable interface between litigation and the other efforts of the Association.

Having reviewed the facts and the issues, the attorney suggested five possible approaches to improving the Pennhurst situation. With relevant statutory and judicial citations, he listed the following alternatives:

1. *The grievances of individual residents.* The Pennhurst study had disclosed cases of abuse, injury, and death to individuals and instances of improper placement and treatment. These cases, Gilhool said, lent themselves to litigation for damages and other relief, but he said the court actions were most appropriately brought by individuals rather than the Association. He therefore recommended that county associations (PARC chapters) should assist Pennhurst residents and their families to invoke existing law for their protection. Such continuing efforts, he said, would have a significant impact on the performance of the state institution.
2. *The misdirection of the present capital plan.* With dismay, PARC had taken note of plans for substantial expenditures for

new construction of institutional facilities. Litigation to prevent major capital expenditures would help focus on the desirability of alternative ways of providing services for the retarded, Gilhool acknowledged, but he noted that PARC had already succeeded in persuading state officials to hold the capital budget in abeyance.[1]

3. *Involuntary servitude.* Mentally retarded residents of Pennhurst were performing maintenance tasks without pay, in apparent violation of the Thirteenth Amendment to the United States Constitution, and an Anti-Peonage Bill had already been drafted. On the theory that at least some of the labor was not beneficial to the resident but rather was necessary to keep the institution functioning, the attorney thought there would be basis for court action. If successful, he said, such action would make it impossible for the institution to operate as in the past.

4. *The right to education.* Citing the decision of the Supreme Court of the United States in *Brown v. Board of Education,* Gilhool said the individual's right to educational services has been recognized by the courts and would seem to override the exclusionary provisions of Pennsylvania's Education Code with regard to certain retarded children. The Code (24 Purd. Stat. Sec. 13–1375) excepts "uneducable" and "untrainable" children from the responsibility of the schools, Gilhool noted, and consigns them to the Department of Public Welfare for "care, training and supervision." He suggested that a suit might be brought with two classes of residents at Pennhurst: (a) those residents traditionally called "educable" but not receiving instruction, and (b) those labeled "uneducable" but not considered so in modern educational concept. The first class would base its case on the Constitutional right of equal protection; and the second class could cite both equal protection and vagueness, in that the categories "uneducable" and "untrainable" are not real and the state has an obligation to educate children who have been placed in those categories. "The impact of such a suit upon the program of Pennhurst is clear," Gilhool asserted; "further it would advance, beyond Pennhurst and even out of the residential context, a central thrust of the Association."

[1]Although PARC decided, following Gilhool's recommendation, to pursue the avenue of a lawsuit on the right to education, the Association continued to work aggressively on the problem of suitable residential services for mentally retarded persons. It hailed with enthusiasm Governor Raymond P. Shafer's statement, in May 1970, that "what Pennsylvania needs is a complete redirection of its services to the mentally retarded during the 1970's." In the statement, which was written with PARC's cooperation, the Governor proposed the development of a statewide network of small, community-based residences. A few months later (November 1970), in pursuance of this idea, the Governor's budget transferred over $21 million from capital expenditures for institutional care to the development of alternative residential and community resources.

5. *The right to treatment.* Cases in the field of mental health had already made the point that an involuntary resident of a state institution is entitled to treatment, else he is being deprived of his liberty without due process. Although the courts recognized the right to habeas corpus, Gilhool commented, they were reluctant to enter the area of determining what adequate treatment might be. Cases based on the issue of right-of-treatment, he said, would require individual suits and would therefore be expensive in time and other resources.

On the basis of his analysis, Counsel Gilhool recommended action on the fourth alternative: right to education.[2] PARC's Legal Action Committee, under the leadership of L. Steuart Brown and the Association's Executive Committee, accepted Gilhool's recommendation and authorized him to proceed.

Strategy and Tactics

As PARC President Wilson put it, the basic assertion of fact, which had to stand up in court if the case was to be successful, was this: that all retarded youngsters, regardless of what traditional label might be attached to them, can benefit from training and education. This was the core and the nub of the case; professional educators understood it, parents wanted to believe it, and if the court would accept it, all else would follow.

Early in 1972, at a regional meeting of representatives of ten state associations for retarded children, Gilhool listed the questions counsel must ask and answer in every case similar to the one in Pennsylvania:

—Who are the plaintiffs?
—Who are the defendants?
—What is the appropriate court?
—What are the causes of the action? How do I write the complaint?
—What information must I gather?
—What expert witnesses shall I enlist, and how shall I use them?
—What role does negotiation play? How do we handle it?

[2]In a subsequent comment, Gilhool observed: "My recommendation for [litigation on] education over [a case confronting] treatment was based on three things: (1) The courts were at home with talk about 'education', but not with talk about 'treatment', and thus chances were better. (2) 'Education' affected a larger number of people than treatment of those involuntarily in institutions. (3) Education in the community is a necessary condition of dismantling the institutions."

—What relief do I ask for? What do we want the court to say?
—What is appropriate implementation after the court issues its order?

These questions, implying strategic and subtle decisions, represent an outline of the Pennsylvania "Right to Education" case, as well as a guide to future cases.

As Counsel Gilhool proceeded to marshall his case during 1970, he and PARC enlisted the involvement of knowledgeable and influential organizations, among them the Council for Exceptional Children, the National Education Association, the American Association on Mental Deficiency, the President's Committee on Mental Retardation, the Harvard Center for Law and Education, and of course the National Association for Retarded Children.

Implied in the original decision to bring the "Right to Education" case was the fact that it would be a *class action.* This was true in two senses: the plaintiffs were to represent the "class" of all retarded persons excluded from schooling; and the defendants were to be the "class" of educational and other public agencies obliged, as PARC saw it, to provide services.

In the selection of plaintiffs, PARC made contact with hundreds of families and presented scores of children's names to the attorney. He reviewed the cases, interviewed dozens of parents, and selected 13 as the plaintiffs. As finally included in the formal complaint, they included 9 males and 4 females, ranging in age from 7 to 20 years and in reported IQ from under 20 to 70. Two were residents of Pennhurst; the others were in community educational programs at their parents' expense or in none at all. In addition to the 13 retarded persons, "on behalf of themselves and all others similarly situated," there was one more plaintiff: the Pennsylvania Association for Retarded Children.

The list of defendants specified in the complaint started with the Commonwealth of Pennsylvania and included the Secretary of Education, the State Board of Education, the Acting Secretary of Public Welfare, and 13 named school districts, "on behalf of themselves and all other school districts similarly situated."

Not every case offers so many choices, but in this instance the attorney could have brought the suit in state or Federal court, and in any of several jurisdictions. For a variety of reasons, in which not only the legal issues but politics, personalities, and other considerations played a part, he and his clients elected to bring the case in the United States District Court for the Eastern District of Pennsylvania. The choice of a Federal rather than state court later gave rise to a challenge, which the court rejected.

Another important decision Gilhool and his clients made at an early stage was to request a three-judge court. In the Federal system, the District Court, the lowest level of the three-tier structure, usually has a single judge sitting in a case. If a constitutional challenge to state statutes is serious and substantial, however, a three-judge court must be convened.[3] Gilhool requested such a court; the Commonwealth of Pennsylvania contended that the challenge of constitutionality was not serious; and Judge Thomas A. Masterson invited argument on the question.

The 22-page plaintiffs' memorandum, prepared by Gilhool, rested principally on the claim that the Pennsylvania statutes and regulations violated the "due process" and "equal protection" clauses of the Fourteenth Amendment to the United States Constitution. These, counsel asserted, were indeed serious and substantial claims and therefore required a three-judge court to adjudicate. The memorandum cited numerous Federal court decisions, including the Supreme Court in *Brown v. Board of Education,* to persuade the court on the merits of the issue. It challenged the constitutionality of several provisions of the Pennsylvania School Code and in several different contexts referred to the denial of rights, the importance of education, and the right of "full due process." Children, the memorandum asserted,

constitute a discrete and insular minority unable to protect their interests by participating in the usual political process and are, therefore, subjects for special protection by the judiciary. Retarded children, regarded historically with prejudice and subjected to discrimination, even more certainly constitute a discrete and insular minority. . . . This, too, requires strict scrutiny of the classifications here challenged.

Despite the opposition of the State's attorney general, representing the defendants, the court found that the plaintiffs' claims raised serious and substantial questions. Judge Masterson thereupon approved the plaintiffs' request and assigned the case to a three-judge court.

Three national organizations respected for their concern with mental retardation and the education of handicapped children early expressed their interest in the case, and Gilhool encouraged them to enter as *amici curiae.* They were the American Association on Mental Deficiency, the Council for Exceptional Children, and the National Association for Retarded Children. In addition to their

---

[3]The days of the three-judge court as a litigatory tactic may be numbered. In his "Report on Problems of the Judiciary" to the American Bar Association meeting in San Francisco on August 14, 1972, Warren E. Burger, Chief Justice of the United States, reported "an unprecedented explosion of litigation," and as part of the remedy he recommended, "We should totally eliminate the three-judge district courts."

substantive contributions, the attorney felt that their involvement would help demonstrate to the court the importance of the Pennsylvania case.

The Council for Exceptional Children, as the nationwide organization of professionals in special education, had been working on the issue of educational opportunities for the handicapped for a long time.[4] Information collected by CEC over the years helped provide a data base for the Pennsylvania case, and authorities recommended by the Council helped establish the principle of educability of all handicapped children.

The Issues in the Case

The principal issue put to the court, in Gilhool's formulation, dealt with equality of *access* to education for the retarded, rather than the *quality* of the education. He put it this way, recognizing that judges are loath to impose requirements or set standards in subject areas that they perceive as being outside their official competence. The attorney had seen courts express a willingness to require the provision of equal opportunity but a reluctance to specify what might be "adequate" or "high-quality."

Exclusions, postponements, waiting lists, and excusals were frequently employed to keep mentally retarded children out of the public schools of Pennsylvania, L. Steuart Brown later recalled. Mr. Brown, who had been education chairman of PARC's Montgomery County Chapter and later of the state association, subsequently served as chairman of the Legal Action Committee of PARC, which was the continuing liaison mechanism for the attorney handling the litigation. In a subsequent account to representatives of state associations from throughout the Northeast Region of NARC, who met in Philadelphia early in 1972, Brown cited the following excuses among those given by public school officials for excluding mentally retarded children:

—We do not have classes for retarded children.
—We do not have room for your retarded child in our class.
—We do not accept retarded children until they are eight years old.
—We do not accept retarded children who have not reached a mental age of five years.
—We do not have classes for junior or senior high age retarded children.

---

[4]See Appendix B, "Basic Commitments and Responsibilities to Exceptional Children." Also Trudeau (1971), Weintraub *et al.* (1971), and *Exceptional Children, passim,* as cited in References.

—We do not accept retarded children who have not been toilet trained.

—We do not accept retarded children who are behavior problems.

—We do not accept retarded children who have multiple handicaps.

—We do not have pre-school classes or kindergartens for retarded children.

—We do not accept retarded children who are not ambulatory.

—We do not have enough money to provide classes for retarded children.

—We shall put your retarded child on our waiting list.

—We are going to exclude your retarded child.

—We shall terminate our program for other retarded children if you make trouble for us.

—We are going to postpone your retarded child's admission.

—We are going to excuse your retarded child because he can no longer benefit from our program.

In organizing the case, in enlisting the expert witnesses, in preparing the documents, and in presenting the evidence, Gilhool kept constantly in mind that he was not simply addressing the court; he was communicating also, in a longer-range sense, with the general public, the mass media, the members of the legislature. This awareness was part of the larger strategy that determined the pattern of the effort, beyond the specific statutes, Constitutional provisions, regulations, and administrative practices that formed the ostensible body of the case.

The attorney recognized that it was necessary to put a large body of information into the case record. He labored to present clear and complete definitions of "mental retardation" and "educability" in order to lay the groundwork for the principle that every retarded child can benefit from education. He also gathered and put on the record in court whatever previous statements he could find from official Commonwealth sources regarding the potentialities of handicapped children. Strong assertions along these lines had been incorporated in departmental reports, in the 1965 comprehensive state mental retardation plan, in proposals under the Federal Developmental Disabilities Act, and in applications for funding grants. The defense naturally found it difficult to contest statements taken from its own published documents.

The complaint, filed in U.S. District Court January 7, 1971, made its points in 134 legally proper and concise numbered paragraphs. After the formal invocation of jurisdiction, enumeration of the parties, and recital of class action allegations, the complaint recited

the facts on which the suit was based. Under the arresting heading
"The Non-Education of Nancy Beth Bowman," the argument recited:

14. Nancy Beth Bowman, born December 12, 1950, has been assigned an
intelligence quotient of approximately 55.

15. From 2-1/2 to 6 years of age, Nancy Beth Bowman at her parents'
expense attended private school from 9:00 A.M. to 2:00 P.M., five days a
week at the Chestnut Hill Rehabilitation Center. Later, she attended the Day
School of the Montgomery County Association of Retarded Children.

16. During this early schooling Nancy Beth Bowman learned the
rudiments of reading and counting; she became toilet trained and learned
table manners.

17. When Nancy Beth Bowman was eight years of age, the school
psychologist of the Abington School District announced that she could not
stay in school and recommended long term placement to her parents. Her
parents have not been informed by the School District whether she was
excluded or excused from the public schools.

18. Since her placement at the Pennhurst State School in 1960, Nancy
Beth Bowman has received no educational instruction, nor is any now being
provided.

And so the complaint proceeded, its impact mounting with the
cumulative rhythm of a bolero, through "The Non-Education of
Linda Taub, . . . of Charles O'Laughlin, . . . of Christopher John
Kelly," and so on through ". . . Glenn Lowrey" (paragraphs 88–91).
The circumstances varied—age, sex, "assigned intelligence quotient," past educational experience, level of development, present
status—but in every case the conclusion was essentially the same:
the retarded child had been denied access to education.

The complaint then changed its focus from the individual
children to the main issue:

92. Education is the central function of American state government. . . .

96. The opportunity of education, where the state has undertaken to
provide it, is a right which must be made available to all on equal
terms. . . .

101. Whatever the traditional label, retarded children of any intelligence
quotient are capable of benefiting from education. . . .

104. Education is even more important to the development of the retarded
citizen than it is to the normal citizen, for the latter may develop skills
willy-nilly and informally, but the retarded citizen cannot, without
sustained educational attention.

105. Education is even more important to the retarded citizen than it is to
the normal citizen, for absent education the retarded citizen will be unable
to provide for himself and will be in jeopardy of institutionalization and loss
of his liberty or, absent education, he may be incapable of self-care and in
jeopardy even of life.

106. The earlier a retarded child begins his education the more thoroughly he will benefit from it and the greater the likelihood of his realizing a capacity for self-sufficiency.

In six counts, then, the complaint charged that specific sections of the Pennsylvania Public School Code deprived the plaintiffs of equal protection of the law and others deprived them of procedural due process of law, both in violation of the United States Constitution, and that certain regulations of the State Board of Education were unlawful and contrary to the Public School Code.

The complaint thereupon asked that the court convene a three-judge District Court, declare specified sections of the Public School Code unconstitutional, enjoin the defendants from enforcing the discriminatory provisions, and require the Secretary of Education to provide for the education of retarded children *in each school district* and *in each State School and Hospital.* The plaintiffs also asked the court to affirm the right of parents to *hearings* with reference to educational placement of their children.

How the Case Proceeded

The case was filed in the Federal District Court January 7, 1971. On June 18, the three judges signed a court order requiring that before any school-age child's educational status is changed, written notice must be given to the parent or guardian. The rights of the child and of the parents are spelled out in the court order, including the right to examine all school records, the right to an independent evaluation of the child, and the right to a hearing. The terms of the court order of June 18 were worked out between attorneys for the plaintiffs and the State.

The "class action" itself—that is, the case of the *Pennsylvania Association for Retarded Children, Nancy Beth Bowman et al. v. Commonwealth of Pennsylvania, David H. Kurtzman et al.*—then went to preliminary hearing before the three-judge court in Philadelphia on August 12, 1971. The schedule called for two days of testimony and cross-examination. Seven expert witnesses were assembled by counsel for the plaintiffs. They were, in the order in which they appeared:

1. I. Ignacy Goldberg, professor of education in the Department of Special Education, Teachers College, Columbia University; secretary of the International Association for the Scientific Study of Mental Deficiency; and past president of the American Association on Mental Deficiency.

2. James J. Gallagher, director of the Frank Porter Graham Child Development Center, University of North Carolina; and former director of the Bureau of Education for the Handicapped and associate commissioner of education, U.S. Office of Education.
3. Donald J. Stedman, professor and chairman of the Division of Human Development, School of Education, University of North Carolina; and former director of the John F. Kennedy Center for Research on Education and Human Development, George Peabody College for Teachers.
4. Burton Blatt, professor and director of the Division of Special Education and Rehabilitation, Syracuse University; and former assistant commissioner and director of the Division of Mental Retardation, State of Massachusetts.
5. Allen C. Crocker, director of the Developmental Evaluation Clinic, Children's Hospital Medical Center, Boston.
6. Jean R. Hebeler, chairman, Special Education Department, College of Education, University of Maryland; president of the Council for Exceptional Children.
7. Gunnar Dybwad, professor of human development, Florence Heller Graduate School for Advanced Studies in Social Welfare, Brandeis University; and former director of the mental retardation project, International Union for Child Welfare.

When the first four had completed their statements, by the afternoon of the first day, it was agreed by attorneys for the plaintiffs and the defendants that no further testimony was needed. The essence of the experts' testimony was to define for the court the term "mental retardation" and its various categories, to indicate the importance of education in the full development of retarded children, and, most important, to support their opinion—with all the prestige that their professional credentials could confer—that every child can indeed be educated. They rejected the IQ as determinative of absolute "intelligence," they decried the use of labels as stigmatizing deviant children, and they maintained that, so far from the schools rejecting children with a mental age below five years, handicapped children even more than others should receive educational services at the earliest possible age. One witness said: "As a special educator, I believe in inclusion of children, not exclusion of children." And another raised the question: "Is it the responsibility of the child to respond to the standards of the school, or is it the responsibility of the school to broaden its range of experiences that it can provide to meet the individual needs of the individual children?"[5] The professional choice of all the witnesses obviously lay in the direction of the latter.

Overnight, spokesmen for the Commonwealth of Pennsylvania consulted with counsel for the plaintiffs and agreed that further testimony would serve no purpose. The two attorneys thereupon joined their efforts to develop a consent agreement, which later received the approval of the court.

[5]Cf. Lauer (1967), Lilly (1970), and Joseph T. Weingold, quoted in Lippman (1972), p. 79.

CHAPTER 5

Outcome of the Case

The consent agreement developed cooperatively by attorneys for the plaintiffs (Pennsylvania Association for Retarded Children, Nancy Beth Bowman *et al.*) and the defendants (Commonwealth of Pennsylvania, David H. Kurtzman *et al.*) included the following salient provisions:

—Having undertaken to provide a free public education to all of its children, including its exceptional children, the Commonwealth of Pennsylvania may not deny any mentally retarded child access to a free public program of education and training.

—It is the Commonwealth's obligation to place each mentally retarded child in a free, public program of education and training appropriate to the child's capacity . . . among the alternative programs of education and training required by statute to be available, placement in a regular public school class is preferable to placement in a special public school class and placement in a special public school class is preferable to placement in any other type of program of education and training.

—The Secretary of Education shall be responsible for assuring that every mentally retarded child is placed in a program of education and training appropriate to his learning capacities, and to that end . . . he shall be informed as to the identity, condition and educational status of every mentally retarded child within the various school districts.

—Insofar as the Department of Public Welfare is charged to "arrange for the care, training and supervision" of a child certified to it, the Department of Public Welfare must provide a program of education and training appropriate to the capacities of that child.[1]

---

[1]This provision was altered in the course of implementation of the decree. A School Administrators' Memorandum issued in the summer of 1972 announced that for a period of one year education would be provided to children in institutions by the Department of Public Welfare, under the supervision of the Department of Education, but thereafter it was to be the responsibility of the Department of Education itself.

—Every retarded person between the ages of six and twenty-one years as of the date of this order and thereafter shall be provided access to a free public program of education and training appropriate to his capacities as soon as possible but in no event later than September 1, 1972.

—Wherever defendants provide a pre-school program of education and training for children less than six years of age, whether kindergarten or how so ever called, every mentally retarded child of the same age as of the date of this order and hereafter shall be provided access to a free public program of education and training appropriate to his capacities.

The consent agreement also required the State to develop a plan for finding retarded children and a plan for providing educational services; it provided for the appointment of Masters to oversee the development of the plans; and it called for notice to parents of retarded children as to the contents of the agreement and court action. The agreement deferred for later consideration the question of what compensatory services should be provided retarded persons 21 years old or more who had been denied education during their minor years.

The court order issued on October 7, 1971, approved and adopted the consent agreement. The three-judge court also enjoined the Commonwealth, the Secretary of the Department of Education, the Secretary of the Department of Public Welfare, and other defendants from the following negative actions, among others: (1) postponing, terminating, or denying any mentally retarded child access to a free public program of education and training; (2) denying tuition and maintenance to any mentally retarded person except on the same terms as applied to other exceptional children. (The intent of this second point was to ensure that children identified as "retarded" would have the same opportunities and financial benefits as those called "brain damaged.")

The whole-hearted acceptance of the terms by the State was emphasized when the Governor, on October 8, appeared at a joint news conference in Philadelphia with officials of the Pennsylvania Association for Retarded Children. Governor Milton J. Shapp was in the first year of his term, having taken office a few days after the filing of the "Right to Education" case. In a statement prepared for the news conference, the Governor said:

This landmark agreement commits the state to a program of identifying, locating, evaluating and placing of all children adjudged to be retarded. . . . In the long run, this agreement will save the taxpayers money because it is a known fact that many children adjudged to be retarded can lead normal and productive lives if given the proper kind of educational assistance early enough. In the short run, this agreement seeks to put as many children as feasible into the public school system.

Governor Shapp's participation in the press conference and his active espousal of the provisions in the consent agreement gave clear evidence that, for practical purposes, the court order, injunction, and consent agreement of October 7, 1971, brought the case to a successful conclusion. There remained, however, some important details to clean up.

Protests and Objections

When, in accordance with the court order, local school districts, parents, and the public were notified of the terms of the consent agreement, protests were entered by local school districts, intermediate school system units, and the Association of Private Schools for Exceptional Children. In formally filed objections and in testimony at hearings November 12 and December 15, 1971, they offered a series of arguments, including:

—The issues do not fall in Federal jurisdiction.
—The case was not properly a class action.
—Local and intermediate school boards were not given due notice of the case; and they were not represented by the Attorney General. (The specifically named defendants in the case had agreed to accept the State's attorney as their legal representative.)
—The consent agreement is unreasonably broad.
—It is not true that all retarded children can benefit from education.
—The consent agreement restricts educational discretion.
—The prior hearing required by the consent agreement would be a remedy worse than the evil it is intended to correct.
—Assignment of a child to a class for the mentally retarded is preferable to the harm that might be done to other children in a regular class by his continued presence there.

In response, attorneys for the plaintiffs and the defendants prepared an amended consent agreement, which led most of the protesting school districts to withdraw their objections. The attorneys then collaborated in the preparation and submission of a memorandum responding to the objections of the Lancaster-Lebanon Intermediate Unit and three of its constituent school districts. Their arguments on the issues of jurisdiction, adequate notice, the principle of educability, and the necessity of due process hearing procedures met with the approval of the court. The objections of the spokesmen for private schools dealt largely with the preferential emphasis given public school facilities; and on this issue too the court accepted the position of the attorneys for the original plaintiffs and defendants, who were by now (November 1971) actively cooperating to implement the consent agreement and the court order of October 7.

The Court's Final Order

On May 5, 1972, all objections having been heard, all appropriate concessions having been allowed, and the terms of the consent agreement being well under way to implementation, Judges Arlin M. Adams, Thomas A. Masterson, and Raymond J. Broderick issued their final Opinion, Order, and Injunction[2] (see Appendix D). The opinion traced in detail the history of the case, recited the plaintiffs' claims and the defendants' and objectors' positions, and interpreted the issues in detail. The court approved and adopted the amended consent agreement that had been formulated by the cooperating attorneys, and applied the provisions to the defendants as a class. The order and injunction reaffirmed and made final the mandate upon the State and its agencies responsible for education and residential care of the mentally retarded to provide equal access to educational services.

As the conclusion to some forty pages of closely reasoned and heavily documented opinion, the judges declared:

In short, we find that both the stipulation and the consent agreement are fair and reasonable to the defendants.

We have absolutely no hesitation about approving the agreements as fair and reasonable to the plaintiffs. Approval means that plaintiff retarded children who heretofore had been excluded from a public program of education and training will no longer be so excluded after September 1, 1972. This is a noble and humanitarian end in which the Commonwealth of Pennsylvania has chosen to join. Today, with the following order, this group of citizens will now have new hope in their quest for a life of dignity and self-sufficiency.

---

[2]The court retained jurisdiction, however, until October 15, 1972, when the final report of the Masters was due on implementation of the consent agreement and order.

CHAPTER 6

Implementation

The consent agreement and the court orders required that the Commonwealth of Pennsylvania search out and find all children requiring special education, whether currently in school or not, and provide the educational services appropriate to their needs. More specifically, the requirements included:

—Notice to the "class of plaintiffs" (that is, to retarded children and their families) through specifically named channels: mailing by the Pennsylvania Association for Retarded Children to each of its chapters; newspaper advertisements by the Department of Justice; delivery to major news media of a joint press release of the parties to the case; and individual notice to each out-of-school child, as he is located, of his newly defined rights.

—Provision to every retarded child of a free public program of education and training "appropriate to his learning capacities." The court order included pre-school programs for retarded children under age six where other children of the same age received public pre-school services. The consent agreement included a mandate for the payment of tuition at day schools or tuition and maintenance at residential schools. Finally, the agreement provided that if a local school district or intermediate unit failed to provide for a retarded child, the Secretary of Education was required to "directly provide, maintain, administer, supervise and operate" the indicated program.

—Periodic reevaluation and right to hearing of all retarded children "not less than every two years."

—Notice to parents before changing the educational assignment of any retarded child; and the right to hearing.

In a sense, implementation of these mandates would be a continuing responsibility, without end. There were, however, deadlines imposed, and the obligation was placed on the Department of Education and the Department of Public Welfare to act quickly.

The tasks, in the few months between the court orders and the fall of 1972, were basically (a) to find the children and (b) to provide them with an appropriate educational program. This statement, however, makes it sound simpler than it turned out to be. *Finding the children* involved mounting a statewide search effort, including extensive publicity through all available media, followed by screening and evaluation, to discover which children would truly benefit from special education programs and precisely what programs were suited to their individual needs. *Providing the educational program* proved to be the end-step of a complex process that involved developing appropriate curricula and teaching materials, recruiting and training personnel, financing the new and expanded programs, finding suitable space, arranging transportation, and many other tasks of planning and administration.

In their effort to carry out the orders of the court within the prescribed time limits, the Pennsylvania Departments of Education and of Public Welfare had the stimulation, guidance, and assistance of two Masters appointed by the court in October 1971. These were:

1. Herbert Goldstein, Ed.D., director of the Curriculum Research and Development Center in Mental Retardation and professor of education in the Department of Special Education, Yeshiva University, New York.
2. Dennis E. Haggerty, member of a Philadelphia law firm, former chairman of the PARC Residential Services Committee, and a consultant to the President's Committee on Mental Retardation.

The role of the Masters was to represent the court in seeing that the orders and injunctions were carried out. Goldstein accepted principal responsibility for the professional review of educational plans, and Haggerty checked the legal implications and represented the concern of Pennsylvania's parents of the mentally retarded. Both were conscious at all times that what they and the State departments were doing would have nationwide and long-term effects.

Although close deadlines were imposed—such as 30 days from the date of the order for the formulation of the plan to find the children, 90 days to identify and locate them, and so on—the objections of interested parties and the additional hearings in

November and December 1971[1] made it necessary to extend the time limits. Nevertheless, the Masters were able to report to the judges in a letter dated May 26, 1972, that the Commonwealth had divided the court's order into two phases and that implementation was going forward.

Phase I (COMPILE) involved the Commonwealth's plan to identify, locate, and evaluate mentally retarded children. This plan, Haggerty wrote the judges, had been presented to the Masters, who had approved it. He anticipated completion by June 30, 1972.

Phase II (COMPET) related to the Commonwealth's plan to educate and train mentally retarded children. Implementation of this phase, the letter said, would have to await the conclusion of Phase I and it might therefore be necessary to request of the court an extension of the time necessary to evaluate Phase II.

As the Commonwealth's written manual correctly noted,

While these plans are separate by title, they both relate directly to providing prescriptive and individualized benefit to mentally retarded children, and should be considered as interfacing portions of an overall educational delivery process. . . . COMPILE is the starting point for COMPET. . . . The prime intent of COMPET is to offer process standards. The actual content, such as individual objectives, methods and material selection is the responsibility of each program.

COMPILE

Within weeks after the promulgation of the consent agreement and the first court order, the two State departments had on paper first drafts of the "Commonwealth Plan for Identification, Location and Evaluation of Mentally Retarded Children" (COMPILE). In published form, the plan ran to 16 single-spaced pages plus eight appendices full of operational details. It called for a multi-agency and multi-disciplinary effort on the part of the Commonwealth to find, assess, and develop programs for the mentally retarded children of Pennsylvania. Task forces were to be established at the State and local levels, including representatives of the appropriate governmental agencies and consumer/citizen representatives.

The evaluation process was defined in detail, including the proper use of assessment forms by the Department of Education and its constituent units. Responsibilities in the assessment process were also specified for the Department of Public Welfare and the Department of Health. At the local level, the plan specified that members of the evaluation team should meet in conference with the

[1]See preceding section, pages 33–34.

County Mental Health and Mental Retardation Administrator to plan alternative education and training programs for children whose recommended placement was other than a public or approved private school.

Parents were to be notified of services available to them through the County Mental Health and Mental Retardation Program Office, which must be prepared, at the request of the parent or guardian, (1) to incorporate the education and training plan into a total plan of life management services for the child; (2) to help obtain for the child additional services not included in his education and training program;[2] (3) to arrange for assistance and consultative services to the home, to the school, and to the child's teacher "as necessary for the child's progress toward the highest possible educational placement"; and (4) to serve as coordinator of all services for the child.

The actual locating of retarded children was a many-pronged effort. Major responsibility was placed on school district superintendents and intermediate unit executive directors, who were to search the records for all children with birthdates from 1950 forward, in order to identify all those retarded or thought to be retarded who were not currently enrolled in school. Follow-up procedures were elaborated in detail.

A separate appendix itemized considerations in the evaluation process, listing specific techniques and instruments to be used in each subject area. Typical of the cautionary comments were these paragraphs:

The evaluation process should include all sources of information which contribute to a thorough understanding of the child. Overdependence upon a limited number of assessment techniques or information sources should be avoided.

Input from parents constitutes a singularly important phase of the evaluation process. . . .

Careful consideration should be given to the attenuating conditions arising from cultural and educational disadvantage, bilingual home conditions and other social, economic and cultural factors affecting the child. These conditions should be taken into account both in the choice of the assessment techniques to be used and in the implications ascribed to the findings.

[2]This addition to the responsibilities of Pennsylvania's county MH and MR offices resembles the functioning of California's Regional Diagnostic, Counseling, and Service Centers and Connecticut's regional centers. See Schmickel, "The Connecticut Regional Approach," in Jones (1968), pp. 379–388, and Lippman, "California Confronts Its 'Undeveloped Resource'," ibid., pp. 389–400.

Publicity was the tool used on the most massive scale to find retarded children. Although it operated in shotgun fashion, it was aimed at many different sub-targets of the Pennsylvania population. The state task force developed the detailed publicity plan and did most of the technical work of carrying it out, with considerable assistance and cooperation from PARC. Supportive efforts by professional groups, unions, and civic and neighborhood organizations also helped promote public awareness.

From the first news release that followed the consent agreement and court order of October 7, 1971, the full publicity power of the Governor's office was utilized in support of the search. As he had in October, the Governor promptly issued a statement following the court's final order in May 1972, expressing his pleasure at the outcome of the case. One week later, on Friday, May 12, 1972, the Governor, the Secretary of Education, the Secretary of Public Welfare, and the Attorney General appeared together at a public meeting in Harrisburg, the state capital, to "help clarify responsibilities for protecting the right of every child to a free public education." It is rarely indeed that four such high officials make a joint appearance at any event in any state; for these officials to convene a public meeting on education of the mentally retarded was surely without precedent.

Throughout May and June the publicity poured out through many channels of communication. Typical of the radio and television spot announcements was this:

In Pennsylvania today all retarded children are entitled to receive a free public education. You can help locate all retarded children under 21 who are not now receiving a regular education. If you are the parent or friend of such a child, write to your local school district or call collect, 717–787–3990. Your helping hand may assist a mentally retarded child receive a good education.

Television films and radio tapes were produced and distributed to broadcasters throughout the state. Check mailings to public assistance recipients included an "envelope stuffer" announcing the search for retarded children. The Liquor Control Board enclosed announcements in consumer packages. Other aspects of the public information plan, as outlined in COMPILE, called for letters from the Governor to Pennsylvania's Senators and Representatives asking them to include the "child search" in their letters to constituents; special Sunday newspaper features; and separate releases on what the individual departments were doing. During the same period, PARC conducted a "Child Hunt" campaign through its chapter communications system and other channels. PARC developed a kit, which it distributed widely, including fact sheets on the consent agreement, suggested speeches for parents, news releases, posters, and automobile bumper stickers. All children located through public agency, PARC, and other efforts were put in touch with the school system.

As of September 1, 1972, the search turned up 8,000 children in the community and 3,000 in institutions with partial or no educational services appropriate to their needs. Of those discovered in the community, it was noted that 52% were mildly or moderately retarded, indicating that the bulk of the out-of-school children were not, as some had thought, the severely and profoundly retarded.

COMPET

Far less dramatic, less easy to implement, and ultimately of greater significance was the "Commonwealth Plan to Educate and Train Mentally Retarded Children" (COMPET). The estimate originally offered by the plaintiffs in the court case suggested some 53,000 retarded children of school age who were not receiving appropriate education. Whether the State plan to locate and evaluate the children would ever find that many, it was clear that a huge new task lay before the special educators and administrators of Pennsylvania.

There were the children, over a wide age-range from pre-school to 21, who would be found out of school. There would be many others in regular classes or otherwise inappropriately placed within the school system. There would be some retarded children in private educational settings whose parents would now want to take advantage of the mandated public services. And there would be those children so severely retarded, or multiply-handicapped, that they would put new, unfamiliar strains on the resources of the schools, or they might be totally unable to leave their homes. For all of these, the State Department of Education and the local school districts and intermediate units now had to develop instructional programs and related services.

The thinking of the Department of Education was reflected in the COMPET draft as it went through successive revisions and refinements in the spring and summer of 1972. The introductory section included this statement of principles:

Education is a life-long process that relates to human development. We can, therefore, consider education as applicable to the infant as well as the adult; the profoundly retarded child as well as the mildly retarded child. To facilitate the realization of a child's potential and our measurement of his development, it is necessary to establish a common denominator which can

We're mentally retarded children, thousands of us, and we're not getting formal education or training.

Maybe our parents, relatives or guardians don't know that public schools can train us in special classes, or even at home, and this education is free!

But schools can't help us if they don't know where we are.

If you know where we live, please help schools find us. If you can't contact a school, call this number collect:

(717) 787-3990

We'll be grateful.

Pennsylvania Department of Education   April 1972

be understood by all individuals working with the child. Such would serve as a basis for program communication, and provide visible and reproducible measurement. Such a common denominator is perhaps best derived from or manifest in the child's behavior. If we use behavior as an observable, and therefore measurable indication of child development, we can measure the benefit provided by a program of education and training according to a child's behavior. . . .

Without relevant pupil objectives or adequate coordination of staff tasks, programs will not be able to comply with COMPET requirements.

The court-appointed Master with particular competence in special education, Herbert Goldstein, made it clear from the outset that he would not be satisfied with the opening of a classroom, the hiring of a teacher, and the installation of a seat for every retarded child. His concern was for the development of *quality education*, and to this end he sought specifics from the Department. The State agency has the power, and under the court order the duty, to require the provision of quality educational services from school districts and intermediate units.

At the same time, it was clearly not possible, between October 1971 and September 1972 (and even less so between May and September 1972), to develop and put into effect a fully matured plan that would effectively meet the educational needs of each retarded child. The best to hope for would be a basically sound approach, with sufficient flexibility to allow improvement as the effort progressed. Development and inauguration of such a program required the best thinking of special educators and others from throughout the nation; and the approach taken by the Pennsylvania Department of Education in the spring of 1972 suggested that it planned to use all such resources. Although the Department of Public Welfare continued to be active, and in some aspects of the implementation it was the leader, both the Department of Education and the Attorney General took the position that carrying out the court's orders was essentially an educational task, and therefore the Education Department had primary responsibility. It is noteworthy that the Commonwealth Department of Education established, within its Bureau of Special Education, a new unit designated as the "Right to Education Office."

The Department of Public Welfare was also busy. In addition to its role on the state task force and other cooperative efforts with the Department of Education, it had responsibility for educational services within the state institutions, as well as a statutory relationship with the county mental health and mental retardation administrators. At a departmental conference in August 1972, it posed, among others, the following questions for consideration by its central office and field staff:

—The Department of Public Welfare has been requested to maintain operation of the education programs in the nine state schools and hospitals for state fiscal year 1972–73, "under supervision of the intermediate units [of the State Department of Education]." How will the Intermediate Unit supervise educational programs at the nine state schools and hospitals?

—The Pennsylvania Department of Education may assume total responsibility for education at the nine state schools and hospitals during fiscal year 1973–74. What are the implications of this?

—Who will be responsible for programing before and after school hours?

—Is it possible that parents, since they now have a right to "due process" hearing, may opt to send their children to a state school and hospital rather than a community program? Will more mentally retarded children in fact be admitted to state schools and hospitals as a result of "due process"?

Through the remainder of 1972, the Department of Public Welfare continued to press for county-level action in child-finding and other aspects of implementation of the court order. Under date of December 14, 1972, however, in a report to the Office of Fiscal Management, the director of the Bureau of Consulting Services commented:

Unfortunately, because the request for additional positions submitted in September 1971 and resubmitted in 1972 were not approved, approximately 1,200 school-age individuals continue to receive little or no education and training. Simply stated, the current status of the Right to Education is as follows: We know who the children are, what their needs are, and we are ready to try to meet their needs, but we are in need of additional staff in order to meet the needs of all mentally retarded children.

By mid-summer 1972, it was apparent that, although the State was making full effort and was indeed finding and preparing to educate large numbers of mentally retarded children, the letter of the consent agreement and court orders would not be in full effect by September 1. Finding *every* retarded child and providing *quality* education for all were tasks that would take longer. The Masters anticipated that it might require another whole school year for the first-round implementation effort to shake down. They therefore recommended to the court that it retain jurisdiction beyond what was originally envisioned as the final date of October 15, 1972. With the encouragement of the Masters, the Department of Education built evaluation into the new program for education and training to ensure flexibility and promote rising quality.

Once the basic plan was developed and, the children having been located, the scope of the task was known, there were still four major obstacles to implementation: recruiting teachers and other specialized personnel; training those new employees who were not fully qualified; finding space for all the new classes; and financing. The court and the Masters were not directly concerned with these difficulties, which remained the problems of the Department of Education and other agencies of the State, probably including the Legislature. The court and the Masters continued to watch the actions of the Commonwealth, however, to be sure of compliance with the order.

As of mid-September 1972, thirty hearing officers had been appointed to act for the Secretary of Education in the hearings. Selected jointly by the Right to Education Office and the Pennsylvania Association for Retarded Children, these officers were special educators chosen for their professional experience and their acceptance of the principle of education for all.

Meanwhile, as the government officials at State and local levels proceeded with COMPILE and COMPET, another idea was taking shape in PARC. Before 1971 had ended, the Association had in draft form a plan calling for the employment of a group of "educational advocates" to help parents and guardians secure for their retarded children the right to education and training, which the consent agreement seemed to offer. PARC recognized that, no matter how enthusiastically and how thoroughly the State Department of Education worked to implement the court's "Right to Education" order, there would be an unevenness of administration in the communities of Pennsylvania. To remedy this anticipated inadequacy, the Association proposed to expand its staff by the addition of nine educational advocates and a coordinator, who together would facilitate the development of quality programs of education and would work with PARC chapters and individual parents to ensure that the children receive the services. The court order and the administrative implementation had created, through the mechanism of due-process hearings, an official forum for child advocacy; and PARC proposed to use the new mechanism to the fullest.

CHAPTER 7

Impact and Reverberations

Within hours after the interim court orders of June 18 and October 7, 1971, there were reactions throughout Pennsylvania and indeed nationwide. Press coverage was extensive. In addition to the newspapers and other major media of Pennsylvania, there was an editorial in the *New York Times*,[1] which of course reached interested readers throughout the United States. Commenting with approval on the court order that affirmed the consent agreement, the *Times* editorial pointed to some of the longer-range implications:

The ruling by a three-judge Federal court in Philadelphia that the state of Pennsylvania must provide free public education to all retarded children constitutes a historic step in an area that has suffered from public and professional neglect. Similar court tests will inevitably be instituted elsewhere unless school systems across the country move toward voluntary compliance with what will surely become the universal legal requirement.

The education of retarded children is a difficult task, but it is clearly a responsibility to be borne by school and society. For parents it is, under present chaotic and often callously inadequate provisions, both a personally heartbreaking and financially ruinous problem. School systems apply widely differing standards in categorizing youngsters ineducable. Even where districts nominally accept the responsibility for keeping such children in school, they often fail to provide effective instruction, thus adding frustration to disability. Yet the few existing private institutions of acceptable quality are beyond the financial reach of most families of even comfortable means.

The court ruling is humane and socially sound. Whatever the cost of educating retarded children, the cost of setting them adrift in the world without giving them the means to lead useful lives is far higher. It is also

---

[1]At the time the case was filed, the *New York Times* (January 8, 1971) published a thoroughly detailed account on page one. The editorial appeared October 13, 1971.

morally indefensible. With only about 3 per cent of the school-age population in the retarded category, the nation is surely able to provide the means to point these youngsters on a productive course.

A court order alone, however, is not enough. To translate the law into educational policy requires fully trained personnel and adequate staffing in existing schools and in special facilities. United States Education Commissioner Sidney P. Marland Jr. urges that 1980 be set as the target year for assuring all retarded children of a free public education. The Pennsylvania ruling provides a new legal basis for eliminating a glaring neglect.

In the ensuing months, there was a rising flood of reports and interpretive articles, first in the mimeographed monthly newsletters of local associations for retarded children, then in publications of the Pennsylvania and National Associations for Retarded Children and other periodicals read by parents of handicapped children, and later in professional journals whose readers included educators, other workers in mental retardation, and attorneys. The impact was immediate, substantial, and continuing.

The aggressiveness of the Pennsylvania Association for Retarded Children has already been noted.[2] PARC cooperated with the State agencies in searching out retarded children—but beyond that it planned for monitoring and advocacy functions.

After the court order putting the consent agreement of October 1971 into effect, parents and friends of children with handicaps other than mental retardation quickly saw the even larger implications. If it was indeed fact that the Commonwealth of Pennsylvania and the local school districts must now provide education and training for every child, it was no longer appropriate to reject a child who was emotionally disturbed, cerebral palsied, or otherwise handicapped. Parents began to request services for their exceptional children, and educators began to think of serving youngsters with an ever-widening range of disabilities.

Elated as he was, the attorney for the plaintiffs, Thomas K. Gilhool, quickly warned that court decisions are no more self-enforcing than are statutes. A court order will reinforce an existing law, he observed, but either one—or both—will require follow-up by interested parties. He suggested to leaders of PARC and other interested parties that it would be appropriate to hold training institutes for parents and others who should take on the advocate role.

To multiply the impact of the Pennsylvania decision, even before the final court order was issued, the National Association for Retarded Children convened a Northeast Region Legal Action Seminar at Philadelphia on Saturday, March 11, 1972. Some 43 persons attend-

---

[2] See preceding chapter, pages 39 and 44.

ed, from nine states and the District of Columbia. They included officers, members, and executives of Associations for Retarded Children, attorneys, and university representatives.

At the all-day seminar, the history, progress, and implications of the Pennsylvania case were laid out in detail by spokesmen for PARC who had been actively involved in the case. There were also reports on pending and planned cases in other jurisdictions. The mood, as the day's program concluded, was: "Let's go back home and do the same!"

Even before the meeting in Philadelphia, the interim order of the Federal court was being interpreted as having an effect on educational obligations elsewhere. Within a week, the following statement appeared on page one of a Boston newspaper:

Retarded children in Massachusetts—and across the nation—may have won the absolute right to be educated in public schools as the result of a federal court ruling Friday in Philadelphia. . . .

The impact of the ruling on Massachusetts school systems will be "profound," according to Dr. Gunnar Dybwad, professor of human development at Brandeis University and an international expert on mental retardation.

"The Pennsylvania decision is a clear signal to all authorities, state and local, that the time has come to speedily revise the procedures by which certain students are excluded from the educational process," Dr. Dybwad said yesterday.[3]

On November 3, 1971, the New Jersey Association for Retarded Children wrote to the Governor of that state, the Commissioner of Education, the Attorney General, and the president of the State Board of Education, calling attention to the Pennsylvania case and the court order of October 7. The letter concluded:

This landmark decision makes it discriminatory to deny an education to any child. In view of this, the New Jersey Association for Retarded Children is vitally interested in learning from you whether the State of New Jersey plans to revise its present regulations governing the implementation of the Beadleston Law.

Many thousands of retarded children are now excluded from educational opportunities because of their classification and the arbitrary way in which children are labeled.

We would appreciate hearing from you as to what action New Jersey plans to take as a result of the Pennsylvania decision.

The New York State Commission on the Quality, Cost, and Financing of Elementary and Secondary Education had been working for more than a year on its complex and politically sensitive assign-

[3]"Mass. Schools Alerted on Retarded Ruling," *Sunday Herald Traveler*, October 10, 1971.

ment. In the first volume of its report, issued early in 1972, it dealt principally with the knotty problems of financing, and in the introductory pages it took note of recent court actions:

A word about certain characteristics of our report. The substance of our recommendations has necessarily been profoundly influenced by a series of judicial decisions of great importance; the most significant of these have been handed down during the past year, and some of them are still on appeal to higher tribunals. They bear upon such vital subjects as the financing of education as it affects equality of educational opportunity; racial segregation; aid to parochial schools; and *special obligations of the state with respect to certain handicapped children.* Some of these have literally been landmark opinions which, if upheld, would drastically limit the options of New York State in these areas. The lawyers on the Commission and staff have appraised these decisions to the best of their professional ability. It has been our general purpose to propose changes in New York's educational system which would be essential if the state is to meet judicial standards which we believe to be sound in principle and constitutionally valid. In our view it is better for New York to adopt a plan which meets constitutional criticism of the kind now emerging, rather than be forced to alter its educational system in haste as a consequence of judicial mandate.[4]

In its discussion of "Children with Special Needs," published later in the year, the New York State Commission offered the following as its first recommendation:

The State Education Department should produce a plan to identify all the handicapped children in the state over the next two years and to expand special-education services to meet their needs. An important part of the plan should be identification of the numbers of trained professionals—teachers, psychologists, physicians and so forth—available to serve these children throughout the state.[5]

Reinforcing the theme of the Federal court in the Pennsylvania case, the Council for Exceptional Children, at its fiftieth annual convention in March 1972, adopted the following resolution:

The Council for Exceptional Children reaffirms its belief that every child has the right to an appropriate publicly supported education. The Council for Exceptional Children applauds recent judicial, legislative, and administrative actions which have supported this right.

---

[4]Report of the New York State Commission on the Quality, Cost, and Financing of Elementary and Secondary Education, 1972, Vol. 1, p. v. Emphasis added.

[5]*Ibid.,* Vol. 2, p. 9.18. In a subsequent newspaper article, Manly Fleischmann, chairman of the Commission, wrote: "I had considered myself a reasonably informed citizen, but I simply could not have been made to believe that more than half of our identifiably handicapped children in New York State receive no special education of any kind." ("The Education of Manly Fleischmann," *New York Times* Annual Education Review, January 8, 1973, p. 68.)

We are concerned that there are still children at home and in institutions who have been excluded from the right to an education.

We are concerned that there are many children who have been placed in educational settings without concern for their rights of due process.

We are concerned that there are numerous children desperately needing special educational assistance, who are denied such assistance by the educational system.

The Council for Exceptional Children urges its members individually, and through their chapters and federations, to initiate and support activities to assure children the right to an appropriate publicly supported education.

Other Cases

At the NARC Legal Action Seminar in Philadelphia, L. Steuart Brown, who had a major role in the Pennsylvania case and who was by this time chairman of NARC's Regional Legal Action Committee, told the group there had been inquiries from Tennessee, North Carolina, North Dakota, and even from New Zealand,[6] and he reported that PARC had already received many requests for assistance in starting similar legal action in various courts throughout the United States.

In point of fact, a number of cases were under way even before the interim decision in the Pennsylvania suit. To some extent, they proceeded simultaneously along separate tracks, but there is reason to believe that the consent decree and court orders in the Pennsylvania case either stimulated or encouraged similar thinking on the part of judges elsewhere.

Mills et al. v. Board of Education of the District of Columbia et al. Peter Mills and six other children brought suit, through their parents and guardians, against the Board of Education and the Department of Human Resources of the District of Columbia, alleging that they had been denied public education, and that their exclusion was based on labeling, "without a formal determination of the basis for their exclusion and without provision for periodic review of their status." The children were variously identified as slightly brain damaged, hyperactive, epileptic and mentally retarded, and mentally retarded with an orthopedic handicap. In a stipulation and order issued December 20, 1971, the court called for the provision of education for the named plaintiffs, the identification of other members of the class (children denied or excluded from public educa-

[6]The Fifth International Congress on Mental Retardation, meeting at Montreal, Canada, October 1–6, 1972, had as its theme "The Rights of the Retarded," and although the program had been substantially planned before the Pennsylvania decision was handed down, the case attracted considerable interest among those attending.

tion), and the provision of information as to the number and identification of children so excluded. The President's Committee on Mental Retardation has declared that the final decree in the *Mills* case "significantly expanded the principle of the Pennsylvania case" (*PCMR Message*, November 1972, p. 3).

Even before the court issued its final opinion, the Board of Education of the District of Columbia on February 9, 1972, unanimously adopted a resolution, which contained the following Preamble:

A new Board of Education took office on January 24, 1972. The newly constituted Board believes that everyone is entitled to a free publicly-supported education suited to his needs, regardless of the degree of his mental, physical or emotional disability or impairment, and regardless of where he lives. For those who live in the District of Columbia, providing this education is the responsibility of this Board. Sound educational policy requires the steps which we are taking, and this is the basic reason for our action. While obviously we have considered, among other pressing problems, the pendency in the United States District Court of *Hobson v. Hansen* and *Mills v. Board of Education*, our decisions have been based on sound educational policies and the need for strengthening the educational programs of our school system.

After directing, in considerable detail, compliance with the court order of December 20, the resolution concluded with the following paragraphs:

It is the intention of the Board to submit for approval by the Court in *Mills v. Board of Education* a Memorandum of Understanding setting forth a comprehensive plan for the education, treatment and care of physically or mentally impaired children in the age range from three to twenty-one years. It is hoped that the various other District of Columbia agencies concerned will join with the Board in the submission of this plan.

It is further the intention of the Board to establish procedures to implement the finding that all children can benefit from education and have a right to it, by providing for comprehensive health and psychological appraisal of children and the provision for each child of any special education which he may need. The Board will further require that no change in the kind of education provided for a child will be made against his wishes or the wishes of his parent or guardian unless he has been accorded a full hearing on the matter consistent with due process.

Clearly, the commitment of the Board of Education went far beyond the mentally retarded, and indeed beyond the few specialized handicapping conditions of the seven named plaintiffs in the *Mills* case. Although neither the court order nor the Board of Education resolution has any binding effect outside its own jurisdiction, and they are therefore not "precedents" in a legal or judicial sense, they may serve as persuasive examples to other educational administrators.

Wyatt v. Stickney et al. In Alabama, the attorney, George Dean, chose to pursue the "Right to Treatment" issue, which Gilhool had rejected in favor of "Right to Education" in Pennsylvania.[7] When the case originated, in 1970, it concerned patients at a state mental hospital. Later, it was broadened to include residents of Partlow State School and Hospital, Alabama's only institution for the mentally retarded.

The original case held that a mental patient in a state hospital was entitled to treatment and habilitation, else he was unlawfully incarcerated. If the hospital was seen as a therapeutic institution, it was obliged to offer therapy. The same principle was offered with reference to the mentally retarded in *Wyatt v. Stickney.* Testimony was offered after lengthy tours of inspection by Philip Roos, executive director of the National Association for Retarded Children, and other recognized authorities in the field of mental retardation. They testified that, far from a program of habilitation, the care offered at Partlow was below even minimal standards of simple custody. Roos described the institution as a "long-time warehouse operation . . . primitive and unmanageable . . . a direct threat to the lives of some patients."

In a preliminary reaction to the testimony, the judge ordered immediate correction of safety hazards, poor sanitation, and health practices, and ordered the employment of 300 new attendants within 30 days as an emergency measure. He directed the Alabama Department of Mental Health to go outside the state merit system, if necessary, to hire the additional employees.

Then, in a formal order and decree issued April 13, 1972, the court issued even more sweeping instructions. First, the judge summarized the case and his findings:

Put simply, conditions at Partlow are grossly substandard. . . . The operation of Partlow suffers from a virtual absence of administrative and managerial organization. . . . Unfortunately, never, since the founding of Partlow in 1923, has the Legislature adequately provided for that institution. . . . Atrocities occur daily. . . .

The court thereupon ordered the implementation of a detailed and explicit series of standards, including the provision of habilitation, education, and treatment; the principle of "normalization"; the imposition of "the least restrictive conditions necessary" to achieve the purposes of the program; the provision of suitable educational services "regardless of chronological age, degree of retardation, or

[7]See above, page 22.

accompanying disabilities or handicaps"; prompt and adequate medical treatment; "the right to dignity, privacy and humane care"; freedom from unnecessary or excessive medication; protection against indiscriminate use of physical restraints; and numerous other safeguards. The court order further specified the required staff-resident ratios (separately for mildly, moderately, and severely/profoundly retarded residents) with reference to psychologists, social workers, educators, vocational therapists, recreational therapists, occupational therapists, registered nurses, and resident care workers; and it itemized the ratios of physicians, physical therapists, speech and hearing therapists, dentists, and chaplains for the resident population of the whole institution. In gross, the requirements called for 207 in staff for each 250 residents. The order called for the establishment of a standing human rights committee, to "guarantee" that residents receive constitutional and humane habilitation. "In so ordering," the judge observed severely, "the Court emphasizes that these standards are, indeed, minimums only peripherally approaching the ideal to which defendants should aspire."

As in the Pennsylvania and District of Columbia suits, the Alabama case was heard in Federal District Court. A new element in *Wyatt v. Stickney* was that among the *amici curiae* was the United States of America, represented by the Department of Justice. This was at the instigation of Judge Frank Johnson of the U.S. District Court in Montgomery, who in his comprehensive preliminary order of March 12, 1971, "requested and invited" the Federal Government to appear as *amicus.*

Willowbrook. The largest institution for the mentally retarded in the world is Willowbrook State School in New York. In 1971 it had a capacity of 4,726 and a resident population of 5,201. Those called "profoundly retarded" represented 40% of the residents. The resident/ward-employee ratio was 2.7:1, almost the best it had been since the opening of the facility in 1948. Nevertheless, there was increasingly open criticism of Willowbrook from parents of the residents, from legislators and other visitors, from the press, and even from employees of the institution.[8] Charges included inhumane treatment, inadequate medical and dental care, insufficient and inadequately trained staff, violations of the patients' and their

---

[8]In fact, a group of parents took an additional and unprecedented step, early in 1972, when they brought charges of "crimes against humanity" before the Division of Human Rights of the United Nations. The recently organized Federation of Parents Organizations for the New York State Mental Institutions brought the charges against the Governor of New York, the Commissioner of Mental Hygiene, and other State officials, alleging "maintenance of conditions universally below minimum human standards of decency, habitation and sanitation which have led to hundreds of deaths."

families' rights of due process, unnecessary deaths, pregnancies and births out of wedlock—the whole range of abuses described at Pennhurst, Partlow, and elsewhere around the nation.

This was far from new. Senator Robert Kennedy had visited Willowbrook in 1965 and had called conditions scandalous. Additional funds and staff were made available, but in the ensuing years conditions deteriorated again. Then, in 1972, WABC-TV, Channel 7 in New York, broadcast nightly for several weeks film that had been shot at Willowbrook, augmented by interviews with local and national authorities and film of alternative programs elsewhere. This was not new either; television had covered other state institutions for the retarded. There were, however, three significant differences: (1) The WABC-TV coverage was skillful, honest, and complete. It told the truth, the whole truth. This shocked the average citizen with new knowledge. (2) It was sustained—not merely one brief segment, or one documentary, but a continuing series, which had cumulative effect. (3) Because it was in New York, communications center of the country, it had a nationwide impact. The television networks used some of the film for national news programs. Daily newspapers and national weekly news magazines picked up the story. Senator Jacob Javits and several Congressmen became concerned; the White House expressed interest; a delegation of Federal officials toured Willowbrook and published a highly critical report.

With all this, it might yet have been a flurry and a diminution of interest, as in 1965. But this was 1972. There had been a Pennsylvania "Right to Education" case, an Alabama "Right to Treatment" case, and additional cases were pending or in preparation in other states. After TV and press coverage, after speeches and letters to the editor, and after Congressional visits, there was action.

On March 17, 1972, two separate suits were filed: *New York State Association for Retarded Children et al. v. Nelson Rockefeller et al.* and *Patricia Parisi et al. v. Nelson Rockefeller, individually and as Governor of the State of New York, et al.* The details varied, but the substance was similar to *Wyatt v. Stickney* and other cases already in the courts. In New York too, the plaintiffs took their cases to the United States District Court, alleging violations of rights under the U.S. Constitution. They sought injunctive relief, on a class basis for all 5,200 residents, and the eventual phasing out altogether of Willowbrook State School.

By mid-1972, there were also cases pending in Massachusetts, Tennessee, Georgia, Maine, South Carolina, and Indiana (*PCMR Message*, May 1972; Friedman, 1972). In several of the cases, the *Washington Daily News* reported on April 15, 1972, the U.S. Department of Justice was planning to intervene. Cases of potential "landmark" significance were proliferating so quickly that the Council for Exceptional Children undertook publication of "A Continuing Summary of Pending and Completed Litigation Regarding the Education of Handicapped Children" (Abeson, 1972). The third edition, published in late May, summarized 14 cases under such headings as Right to an Education, Right to Treatment, and Placement. A separate compendium for the Office of Mental Retardation Coordination, U.S. Department of Health, Education, and Welfare, about the same time (Friedman, 1972), also summarized pending cases dealing with "involuntary servitude" and the indefinite commitment of an accused criminal who was found incompetent to stand trial.

Further Ripples

Outside the courtrooms too there were activities and movements toward more equitable opportunities for the mentally retarded and other handicapped children, and, to some extent, handicapped adults as well (Abeson, 1972a). Some of these developments, in 1971–72, were traceable to the Pennsylvania, District of Columbia, and Alabama cases. Others had their origin in the mood and temper abroad at the time. Still others had been resting fallow in the minds of men or in plan-files, waiting to exercise the power of an idea whose time has come.

In Rhode Island, the Legislature enacted a bill extending mandatory public education to severely and profoundly retarded children, effective July 1, 1972. In November 1971, the Rhode Island Association for Retarded Children adopted a series of policy statements indicating how the Association and its nine chapters were to help implement the law.

In New York, the Department of Mental Hygiene inaugurated a series of actions designed to change the pattern of service in the state schools and to result in the development of additional community services. These developments, in 1971 and 1972, were in implementation of recommendations contained in the 1965 New York State Plan for Mental Retardation. Intake was closed at Willowbrook and at other state residential facilities; smaller residential units were opened; review committees were established at the state schools to evaluate the facilities for compliance with nationally recognized accreditation standards; directors of planned state schools that had not yet been constructed (called, derisively, "phantom institutions") found their responsibilities had been re-titled Developmental Services, and, with staffs of limited size but different skills, they undertook to work with county, municipal, and voluntary agencies toward the organization and provision of additional services for retarded persons and their families in the communities.

In New York City, the Board of Education's Bureau for Children with Retarded Mental Development assumed responsibility for 13 classes formerly conducted by the Association for the Help of Retarded Children. Approximately 130 youngsters, called "severely retarded" by the Association for the Help of Retarded Children and previously rejected by the public school system, were now accepted as the responsibility of the Board of Education. In addition to the fully-credentialed teacher and an assistant for each class, plus a head teacher for each unit, the New York City Bureau for Children with Retarded Mental Development undertook to provide psychological services, speech therapy, and social services.

At the same time, in the 1971–72 school year, families and attorneys were making increased use of Sections 4403 and 4407 of the New York State Education Law (Guarino and Sage, 1972); by filing claims and bringing actions in Family Court, they exerted pressure on the New York City Board of Education to establish additional special classes for progressively more severely handicapped children. The Legal Aid Society, which had begun prosecuting cases in behalf of parents of handicapped children for state and local funding of special education services under non-public auspices, issued a detailed description of how to use the provisions of the Education Law and the Family Court Act (Wottitz, 1972) and the *New York Law Journal* (June 22, 1972) gave the information and procedural suggestions even wider circulation among practicing attorneys.

In New Mexico, the Attorney General held that "the state, in our opinion, is required to offer educational opportunities to all the children in the state." In reaching this conclusion, he cited *Brown v. Board of Education* (1954), *Hobson v. Hansen* (1967), and the consent agreement in *Pennsylvania Association for Retarded Children v. Commonwealth of Pennsylvania* (1971). He ruled that New Mexico's special education laws, previously considered permissive, were in fact mandatory.

In California, the Department of Mental Hygiene developed statewide regulations to assure protection of the civil rights of the mentally retarded and the mentally ill, in accordance with provisions of the innovative Lanterman-Petris-Short Act.

At the national level too there were developments attributable at least in part to the innovative court actions and resulting decisions. A National Center for Law and the Handicapped was opened at South Bend, Indiana, in 1972. Financed by a grant from the Department of Health, Education, and Welfare, it is sponsored by the Family Law Section of the American Bar Association, the National

Association for Retarded Children, Notre Dame University, and the Council for Retarded Children of St. Joseph County, Indiana.

The United Cerebral Palsy Associations, Inc., in the June-July 1972 issue of its legislative newsletter, *Word from Washington,* reported:

> Because of the Pennsylvania Right to Education Consent Decree, pressure is mounting in Congress for major Federal funding to states for education of the handicapped. Several bills have been introduced. Since the Pennsylvania Consent Decree required the Pennsylvania Department of Education to provide a free public educational program for *all* retarded children regardless of the severity of their retardation . . . State governments face prospects of litigation and court orders to serve scores of unserved or poorly served handicapped children. In order to meet the requirements of the courts, state budgets for education of the handicapped will have to be significantly supplemented.
>
> To meet this newly enforced responsibility of the states to serve the handicapped, Senator Harrison Williams introduced S. 3614 which would authorize federal payments to state and local school boards beginning in FY '73. The federal government would pay 75% of the additional costs of educating a handicapped child. The program is estimated to cost $400 to $800 per child per year, in additional Federal funds.
>
> The Williams bill also reaffirms the right of handicapped children to education, requires the identification of all handicapped children, and seeks statewide evaluation and reform of all current educational programs, including institutional programs.
>
> Other sponsors of S. 3614 include Sen. Magnuson and Sen. Randolph.
>
> In a related drive in the House, Rep. Koch and Rep. Brademas introduced an amendment to the Education of the Handicapped Act (H.R. 15034) to provide direct federal funding to public and private institutions serving the severely and profoundly retarded. The Koch/Brademas proposal targets the education of the very severely retarded. The measure is responsive to specific incidents and exposés of institutions recently.

Also at the Congressional level, Senator Jacob Javits (New York), for himself and 21 other Senators, introduced a measure (S. 3759) that he called "Bill of Rights for the Mentally Retarded." The bill, which ran to 221 printed pages, specified in great detail the standards that state residential facilities for the retarded must meet if they were to receive Federal funds authorized by the measure. As strong and progressive as the bill seemed on first reading, a number of letters from organizations concerned with mental retardation urged that there be more explicit and more extensive reference to the need for education and other services at the community level *(Congressional Record,* June 28, 1972).

As a guide to further action at the state legislative level, the Council for Exceptional Children published "A Model Law for the Education of Seven Million Handicapped Children" (Weintraub *et al.,* 1971, pp. 110–142).

CHAPTER 8

Implications for Education

The Bureau of the Census reported that in 1969 about 450,000 children between the ages of 6 and 15 were not enrolled in school. (This total does not include youngsters in institutions, which would bring the figure higher.) They were mentally retarded, physically crippled, emotionally disturbed, non-English speaking, or had some combination of disabilities that led the public schools to exclude them (President's Committee on Mental Retardation, *MR 71*, p. 16). For the same year, the Bureau of Education for the Handicapped asserted that 3,751,571 handicapped children—62% of the national total—were not receiving special education services. The decisions of the Federal courts in the Pennsylvania and other "Right to Education" cases will change this inequity.

What the U.S. District Court said in *Pennsylvania Association for Retarded Children, Nancy Beth Bowman et al. v. Commonwealth of Pennsylvania, David H. Kurtzman et al.* in 1972—as the Supreme Court of the United States had said in *Brown v. Board of Education* in 1954—was that the state and its agencies must provide educational services for every child. Whatever the degree of handicap, wherever the child is, whatever his educational needs, the state shall not "postpone, terminate or in any way deny to any mentally retarded child access to a free public program of education and training" (see Appendix D).

The breadth of the language was promptly interpreted to apply to all handicapped children (*The Exceptional Parent*, April-May 1972, p.6). The United Cerebral Palsy Associations, Inc., in a memorandum from its Washington office dated March 10, 1972 (even before the court had issued its final order), commented: "Although the Pennsylvania [consent] decree is specific for retarded children in Pennsylvania it opens the door for an appropriate educational experience at public expense for all children in all states (including cerebral palsied children). States have been alerted that where their laws do not guarantee a free education for all children and do not provide for 'due process' in school placement decisions affecting the handicapped, they are in violation of the equal protection clause of the Fourteenth Amendment."

The "due process" provision of the Federal court decision is as important as any other aspect of the Pennsylvania case, in the opinion of Thomas K. Gilhool, attorney for the plaintiffs.

"For the first time in American education," Gilhool observed in a personal communication to the authors,

a mechanism is created to assure that the educational program fits the child. The mere fact of a hearing *opportunity* on change in assignment and *every two years* thereafter will of course keep all the field professionals on their toes. There is a new instrument for accountability—to the child, to the parent, to the Secretary of Education, and to the teacher as professional. The right to a hearing creates an extraordinary forum for parents and their associations to express themselves, raise issues, enforce rights, get things done, and *to organize.* Effective operation of due process hearings assumes many things, most notably the existence of informed advocates. It is a forum which should transform the parents' movement. And it should transform education.

The ultimate educational implication is embodied in the expression "zero reject." This concept, which provides in substance that *every child* shall have a place in the educational pattern, has been under consideration for some time, with both proponents and opponents even among special educators (e.g., Lilly, 1970, 1971; Adamson and Van Etten, 1972; Goldberg, 1971). Lilly, who is a major advocate, has defined the student population as the mildly retarded or otherwise handicapped (1970); but the Pennsylvania court order referred to *all retarded* children, and subsequent interpretations are extending the coverage to *all children.*

Not only the total population of children with handicapping conditions are covered, but the whole range also of disadvantaging socioeconomic circumstances. A decade ago, the President's Panel on Mental Retardation (1962) focused on the links among deprivation, mental retardation, and education: "The majority of the mentally retarded are the children of the more disadvantaged classes of our society. . . . A number of experiments with the education of presumably retarded children from slum neighborhoods strongly suggest that a predominant cause of mental retardation may be the lack of learning opportunities." Whereas the President's Panel referred to "a major causative role, in some way not yet fully delineated" (p. 8), a later study entitled *Poverty and Mental Retardation: A Causal Relationship* bluntly itemized a series of social and environmental factors: Poverty and Organic Impairment, The Effects of Cultural Deprivation on Intellectual Performance, Public Education and Mental Retardation: The Self-Fulfilling Prophecy . . . Health . . . Welfare . . . Migrants (Hurley, 1969; see also Allen, 1969, "Legal Rights of the Disabled and Disadvantaged"; and Lippman, 1972, Chapter 10, "What Is a Handicap?").

The overriding implication of the 1971-72 court decisions is the right of equal access to educational opportunity for all children. Dennis Haggerty, who was chairman of the Residential Services Committee when the Pennsylvania Association for Retarded Children began its litigation and who later served as one of the two Masters appointed by the Federal court, put it succinctly: "The real impetus . . . is that there are no slots that children can fall between; that is, education for all means just that, and there is no shifting of responsibility to a department of welfare if the bureau of education feels that child is not educable" *(Mental Retardation News,* January 1972, p.1).

The obligation of the state to educate children in residential facilities for the handicapped had already been acknowledged spottily, even before the Pennsylvania, Alabama, and Massachusetts cases. In the State of Washington, the responsibility of the Department of Education extends into the state residential facilities of the Department of Institutions. This means that classroom standards in institutions are the same as in the public schools in the communities; it also means that teachers must meet the same requirements and receive pay on the same scale as teachers employed by local school districts (Mayeda, 1971, p. 141).[1]

The Accreditation Council for Facilities for the Mentally Retarded (1971), among its first activities after being established within the Joint Commission on Accreditation of Hospitals, adopted standards for educational services in residential facilities for the mentally retarded (Crosby, 1972). Now, with the accumulating record of court decisions, the document offers a set of criteria against which institutional education services can be measured.

Accepting the "developmental model" of mental retardation (Roos, 1970, 1971; Dybwad in *The Exceptional Parent,* April-May 1972),[2] the Accreditation Council (AC/FMR) set forth eight standards, including these statements:

[1] Also see above, pp. 6–7.

[2] Also see below, pp. 70–71.

Educational services, defined as deliberate attempts to facilitate the intellectual, sensorimotor, and affective development of the individual, shall be available to all residents, regardless of chronological age,[3] degree of retardation, or accompanying disabilities or handicaps. . . . The principle that learning begins at birth shall be recognized. . . .

Individual educational evaluations of residents shall commence with the admission of the resident; be conducted at least annually; . . . provide the basis for prescribing an appropriate program of learning experiences for the resident. . . .

There shall be written educational objectives for each resident. . . .

There shall be available sufficient, appropriately qualified educational personnel, and necessary supporting staff, to carry out the educational programs.

Finding the Children

The first responsibility of the public education system is to locate and identify the children not receiving appropriate educational services. The charge to find the children was mandated in the Pennsylvania court order and was promptly initiated through COMPILE.[4] In future cases and in other states, however, the implication will go even further: not only to find those children now at home, who may have been "excused" early or who may never have been admitted to school, but to find and reassign those children who have been incorrectly placed in "regular" classes or in special programs inappropriate to their needs. In classes for the blind, the deaf, the neurologically impaired, the "educable" mentally retarded, the "trainable" mentally retarded, and the "normal," there are children who could learn more effectively under alternate rubrics.

As Herbert Goldstein, professor of education at Yeshiva University and one of the two Masters appointed by the court in the Pennsylvania case, said, it was not enough for the Department of Education to open classrooms and provide teachers; the public school system had the obligation to *seek out* the retarded children who should be in those classes. Moreover, he observed, there was a greater danger of "false positives" than of the opposite. That is, as parents, neighbors, social agencies, and others identified children not currently attending school, there was the possibility that some would be called retarded whose actual disability or handicapping condition

[3]The court, in the Pennsylvania case, left open the question of the obligation of the state to provide educational services for retarded adults. The issue was whether retarded persons who had been denied education during childhood were entitled to "compensatory" service in adulthood. In the Alabama case, the issue was raised whether a retarded person held in custody was not entitled to continuing educational services throughout the period of his residence in a state institution.

[4]See above, pp. 37–41.

might be something else. Even in the routine operation of special education programs in the past, children whose primary problem was a visual or hearing impairment, aphasia or neurological dysfunction, malnutrition or emotional pressure at home, might be incorrectly labeled as mentally retarded and inappropriately placed in an unsuitable educational setting. As the effort was made, in the spring, summer, and fall of 1972, to find, test, and place thousands of out-of-school youngsters, the risk of such inaccurate assessments increased.

In Pennsylvania, as noted, the child hunt was a massive effort. Starting with the Governor's office, it involved two major departments of state government, local school officials and county mental retardation authorities, the Pennsylvania Association for Retarded Children and its affiliated chapters, and the major media of mass communication. Over the longer pull, in states and communities throughout the United States, there could also be involved the community welfare, health, recreational, and civic agencies. Prominent among these would be the PTA as the organization of parents most actively interested and involved in the public schools.

The ultimate target of the child-searching message is the parents of those who should be in school. In reaching them, not only associations for retarded children but organizations concerned with other disabilities can be helpful. There are, for example, organizations of parents using the labels Brain Injured, Learning Disability, or Mongoloid, and some or all these children should be embraced in the new educational policy of equal access.

Finally, the public schools are aware of the value (and the hazards) of using school children as messengers to the parents. Children out of school, and children inappropriately placed, often have siblings; and if the cooperation of the brothers and sisters can be enlisted, they too can serve as part of the child-hunt team.

Testing

In Pennsylvania, the search was for retarded children not attending school. The problem, once a child was located, was to evaluate his abilities and determine the appropriate placement.

As the principle extends to children with other handicaps, and to children currently in school but perhaps wrongly placed, the task of assessment and assignment becomes more complex (Kirk, 1972; Segal, 1967; Jones, 1968, Part I, "Diagnostic Centers and Special Schools").

The greater hazard, again, is not that retarded children will be missed but that children with different learning problems will be mislabeled and misplaced as retarded (Garrison and Hammill, 1971). Jane R. Mercer, in her epidemiologic research in Riverside, California, found a disproportionate number of black and Chicano children identified as mentally retarded. Yet, "when sociocultural differences were held constant, there were no differences in measured intelligence" between black and white children, or between children of Spanish-speaking or English-speaking background. She therefore concluded: "The IQ tests now being used by psychologists are, to a large extent, Anglocentric."[5] Studies in Delaware some years earlier likewise showed ethnic differences that may be attributed to sociological and cultural factors rather than to innate racial variations (Jastak *et al.*, 1963). As Hunt (1969) put it, "Intelligence tests measure learned performance, not innate capacity." (See also Albee in President's Committee on Mental Retardation, 1971b.) A conference on problems of education of children in the inner city developed a short series of recommendations for making the educational system more responsive to the needs of disadvantaged youngsters sometimes called retarded; one of these recommendations was: "Reexamine the present system of intelligence testing and classification" (President's Committee on Mental Retardation, 1970).

Beyond testing, the requirement of the court order in the Pennsylvania case was that every retarded person between the ages of 6 and 21 (and below age 6 in specified circumstances) be provided with "access to a free public program of education and training *appropriate to his learning capacities.*" Although the court did not define the standards of quality of education or appropriateness of assignment, the import of the italicized words is clear: that educational services shall be tailored to the needs and capabilities of the individual child. If the Pennsylvania, District of Columbia, and other cases indeed imply such individualization, the decisions will put a new face on education in the United States.

There is another implication, which may be hoped for, but not taken for granted: The placement of each child in an educational setting "appropriate to his learning capacities," especially if reinforced by periodic evaluation and by the informed consent and cooperation of his parents, can lead to genuine integration of exceptional children into the main body of education. A system responsive to the needs and capabilities of every child should eventually

---

[5]The terminology is that of California, where people of Mexican-American background are called Chicano, and other white people are labeled Anglo. These statements by Mercer are taken from her paper, "Pluralistic Diagnosis in the Evaluation of Black and Chicano Children: A Procedure for Taking Sociocultural Variables into Account in Clinical Assessment," as presented to the American Psychological Association meetings September 3–7, 1971. The material is to be incorporated and elaborated in a forthcoming volume, *Labeling the Mentally Retarded.* See also Mercer in Stedman, 1971, pp. 3–15, and Mercer in Koch and Dobson, 1971, pp. 23–46.

lead him toward learning experiences with his peers and contempo-
raries. As the educational structure becomes more flexible and
responsive to individual needs, the barriers of "special" versus
"regular," "educable" vs. "trainable," "mentally" vs. "neurologically" handicapped, should all come down. Then the educational system will deal with children as people, and each will learn at his own
speed and to his own potential limit.

Cost Implications

Doing something costs more than doing nothing. (Or at least so it
seems. Actually, doing *nothing* for children may entail huge
expenses, in social dependency, as they grow older. *Failing* to educate does not *save* money; it merely *transfers* the expense to the
custodial or correctional institution, to the welfare system, to the
public health resources.) Similarly, providing education for 100,000
retarded children costs more than providing education for 50,000.
Still, it was the Governor of Pennsylvania, Milton Shapp, who quickly predicted, after the consent agreement and the interim court
order, that the decision would *save* the taxpayers money by freeing
thousands of young people from state schools and hospitals.[6]

The Governor was right, of course. Yet there are real and immediate expenditures, above what the Department of Education and other
state and local agencies were spending the year before, to provide
special educational services for a much smaller number of children.

The scope of the unmet need is dramatized in position papers
presented by the Bureau of Child Guidance of the New York City
Board of Education in May 1972. The paper on "The Mental Health
Crisis in our Public Schools" included these figures:

There are only approximately 164 city budget lines for school psychologists, which means there is one psychologist for approximately 10,000
children. Recommended ratio is one per thousand. We have 215 city budget
lines for school social workers, which is one for every 8,000 children. The
recommended ratio here is also approximately one per thousand. With 66
city budget lines for school psychiatrists, this means that there is only one
psychiatrist for each group of 25,000 children. We have had no new budget
lines in any of these categories for many years, although needs have
increased and demands have proliferated. This is the heart of our and your
problem.

The audience for this presentation was the New York State Department of Mental Hygiene, which provides approximately half the
funds for operation of the Bureau of Child Guidance; and the occa-

---

[6]See above, p. 32; also *PCMR Message*, November 1971.

sion was a budget hearing. The problem was obviously not the shortage of psychologists, of social workers, of psychiatrists, but of funds with which to employ these professional specialists.

In a different context, at a conference on the mentally retarded and the law, some two years earlier, New York City's director of mental retardation services said:

> When one confronts the subject of state legislation with respect to services for the mentally retarded and their families, the first and overriding consideration has to be *funds*. I'm not speaking only of appropriations—urgent and essential as the state budget is. Equally important, in an even more basic way, is the *pattern* of funding, the structure or formula by which the state helps to finance services at the local level.

The attorney for the Pennsylvania Association for Retarded Children brushed aside the argument that the Department of Education, the Department of Public Welfare, and the intermediate and local school systems did not have sufficient funds to provide special education for all the retarded, in conformity with the court order. He reacted as a student of the Constitution: if rejecting a retarded child from educational opportunity denies him "equal protection," he said, the state cannot justify it on the basis of limited funds. The responsibility is there; the obligation to provide the funds devolves on public officials at the highest level—the governor and the legislature. As Gunnar Dybwad said in a published interview *(The Exceptional Parent*, April-May 1972, p. 9):

> A department of state government used to excuse itself by saying, "We don't have enough money, so what do you want us to do?" We have to realize that a department, after all, is only an extension of the governor's office. So, maybe the governor has to be held responsible. After all, it is he who in the long run has the residents of an institution in his custody as the chief executive of the state.

Gilhool, the PARC attorney, suggested that one could make a case with members of the Legislature that the cost of education is lower than the eventual cost of institutional care, plus the loss of prospective income retarded persons will earn if suitably trained (and the resulting taxes paid back to the state by those wage-earning retarded persons).

A spokesman for the Council for Exceptional Children put the issue in different terms. "We don't ask for special privileges for handicapped children," he said.

> If in fact, a state does not have sufficient funds to educate all its children, the handicapped youngster must take his share of the cut with the others. If public funds are so limited that all children must go on double shifts, or must attend school for a curtailed year, the same restrictions must be shared

by the mentally retarded and the other children in special programs. But do not expect the exceptional child to bear the whole burden of the state's financial difficulty, Mr. Governor and Mr. Legislator. He'll suffer his share of the burden—but, by order of the Federal courts, *he will no longer carry the whole burden.*

Funding

The financing of special education for exceptional children has been dealt with in the preceding section; but there is another respect in which school financing may be discriminatory, and this too began to come to the attention of courts and legislatures in 1971–72.

Economists have long viewed property taxes as regressive, hitting the low- and middle-income homeowners (and renters) harder than the well-to-do. In most communities of the United States, and under the tax structures of most states, the heaviest portion of the property tax goes to pay for the public school system. One result is that elderly people and others on limited incomes have had to pay an undue portion of their annual budgets for schooling for the young. The tax pattern has been justified partly as necessity (arising out of the division of taxing authority among the Federal, state, and local governments) and partly on the basis that education of the young brings social benefits to the entire community. When real property was the principal index of affluence, a century and more ago, this was an equitable arrangement; today it discriminates against those whose principal asset is their home.

There is, however, an additional objection to the property tax as the major source of funding for the public schools: it puts the heaviest burden on homeowners and renters in districts where the assessed valuation is relatively low and where the school-going population is high. In affluent communities, by contrast, the tax levy per hundred dollars of assessed valuation is lower. Thus, the property owners best able to afford good schools can get them at the lowest cost, whereas low-income people living in poorer districts pay higher rates and receive less in school quality for their money.

This was the issue put to the courts of California by a barrio-dweller in East Los Angeles and 25 other parents; and in August 1971, in *Serrano v. Priest,* the Supreme Court of the State of California held that the property tax was indeed discriminatory and hence a violation of the Fourteenth Amendment to the United States Constitution (Lubenow, 1972). Similar decisions were subsequently handed down by Federal courts in Minnesota *(Van Dusartz v. Hatfield)* and in Texas *(Rodriguez v. San Antonio),* and by a New Jersey Superior Court *(Robinson et al. v. Cahill et al.).* .

The effect of the *Serrano* case in California, and of the others if upheld on appeal to the Supreme Court of the United States, will be to bring about a major revision of the property tax structure for public education in 49 states. (Hawaii, the exception, supports and operates its schools, so that there are no interdistrict inequities.)

The significance of *Serrano* and the other cases was immediately apparent to school officials, budget planners, and legislators throughout the United States.[7] Authorities on school finance, already entangled in one of the most complex and arcane subjects known to modern man, found themselves grappling with a challenge to their entire structure. The New York State Commission on the Quality, Cost, and Financing of Elementary and Secondary Education, which was studying the subject at the time of the Serrano decision, took note of the California, Minnesota, and Texas cases and recommended that the state assume full responsibility for financing the public schools.[8]

In New Jersey, one of the few populous states that still has no personal income tax and many of whose residents earn their livelihood in New York or Pennsylvania, the Tax Policy Committee submitted to the Governor on February 23, 1972, a five-volume report that flatly asserted:

New Jersey's present tax structure is inelastic and regressive. . . .

The effective rate of tax incidence of the present total state-local tax structure is 19.1 per cent for families with under $3,000 a year in income. For those with over $25,000 a year, the effective rate of the total structure is 5.4 per cent.

The Committee recommended reductions in property taxes totaling $863 million a year, of which $607.9 million was to come through state financing of local school costs.[9] The effect would be to equalize, over a period of years, the amount of public money spent throughout the state for the education of each child. On the basis of the Tax Policy Committee's analysis and recommendations, the Governor proposed the imposition of a state personal income tax; the Legislature in its 1972 (pre-election) session rejected the proposal, but the issue remains.

Although the resolution of the issue raised by the courts is not yet

---

[7]The *New York Times*, in its special-section "Annual Education Review" dated January 10, 1972, devoted many columns to the *Serrano* and allied cases.

[8]See above, p. 48. Also see the report of the New York State Commission, Vol. 1, pp. 2.2, 2.3.

[9]The voluminous report of the New Jersey Tax Policy Committee was summarized and interpreted in a seven-part series of articles in the Bergen County *Record*, March 2–10, 1972. Part V, "How and Why the State Would Pay for Schools," appeared March 8, on page A-15.

clear—and in any case it may take different patterns in different states—there is no doubt that legislatures and school officials will be dealing with a substantially new set of circumstances in the next few years. If, as seems apparent, there will be an approximate equalization of the tax burden, this is likely to raise the quality of schooling in the poorest districts of each state.[10] It would appear a safe assumption that the benefits would reach exceptional children as well as those in the regular classes.

It is surely relevant that the Pennsylvania "Right to Education" case and the California, Minnesota, Texas, and New Jersey cases on property taxes all depended in significant measure on the "equal protection" provision of the Fourteenth Amendment to the United States Constitution. It will hardly be possible to revise state and local tax structures and disbursements for schools without recognition of every child's right to equal access to educational opportunity.

There is a sidelight to the issue of public funding of special education that is significant for thousands of families, even though they represent a small minority of the total population of handicapped children. This is the use of public funds to purchase private special-education services. A number of states—California, Connecticut, New Jersey, New York, and Pennsylvania among them—provide state funds for partial or complete payment of special education costs (in some cases including residential costs) under non-profit or proprietary auspices. What started in New York in 1946 as a special enactment for one physically handicapped child was costing the state, by 1972, approximately $14 million a year. In California, the desire to provide alternative options for the family of a retarded child led to the proposal by the Study Commission on Mental Retardation in 1965 that parents should be able to select the school of their choice, and that if it was a non-public facility, the local school district should contribute toward the cost whatever it would have spent for the child in a public class. The concept has received attention more recently in the form of consideration of "education vouchers," not only for the retarded but for all children.

The U.S. District Court in the Pennsylvania "Right to Education" case took cognizance of the issue, when it ordered that the Commonwealth should not deny tuition (or tuition and maintenance) to any mentally retarded person "except on the same terms as may be applied to other exceptional children," and to this end it specified that the term "brain damaged" should be interpreted to include all

---

[10]School officials in affluent communities are concerned lest there be a reverse inequity imposed by the new tax approach. A number of school districts with high property assessments now are providing additional enrichments of program, for exceptional as well as for "normal" children, beyond what state funds would finance.

the retarded. At the same time, the court endorsed the amended consent agreement, which declared:

Among the alternative programs of education and training required by statute to be available, placement in a regular public school class is preferable to placement in a special public school class and placement in a special public school class is preferable to placement in any other type of program of education and training.

CHAPTER 9

Implications for Special Education

The right to education, as enunciated by the courts in Pennsylvania, the District of Columbia, and elsewhere, is a broadened interpretation of the United States Constitution and judicial (as well as administrative) decisions going back many years. The professional in special education must remember, however, that "education" is by no means a synonym for schooling. As Goldberg testified in the hearing before the three-judge court in Philadelphia on August 12, 1971,

Education is a continuous process of developing life skills needed for effective coping with developmental tasks and demands as well as with the environmental tasks and demands. The process of education, so defined, takes place through some structured and some accidental teaching-learning situation, and through various educational agencies in our society. Some examples of educational agencies in our society are the home, church, TV, radio, theater, industrial centers, etc. . . . As an organized effort, we can very well enter the home of the individual, work with the parents, stimulate the child. . . .

The development of appropriate educational strategies and techniques for working with severely and multiply handicapped children embraced by the Pennsylvania case is a huge and continuous task for all workers in special education. It will require all the imagination, innovation, and skill they can muster.

The theoretical groundwork has begun to be laid, over the years (see the comprehensive five-volume compendium edited by Ellis, 1966–1971). What is needed now, and throughout the foreseeable future, is effective pragmatic implementation. This includes identifying, evaluating (and periodically reevaluating) the children, developing techniques and materials to work around their disabilities and build on their assets, and evolving suitable methods of utilizing all the resources of the school and the community to maximum educational effect for the individual child.

The theory and concepts must become quite specific—at the state level (Pennsylvania and 49 others), in the local school districts, and in the classroom (or at the bedside), where the child is. All resources—the teacher, the psychologist, the social worker, the teacher's aide, the recreation specialist, the physical therapist, the speech therapist; books, magazines, chalkboards, audiovisual materials, kinesthetic stimulation, field trips—must be mobilized to the single end: the fullest and most effective education of the individual. As partners with the practicing educators in this task are the universities and colleges of education, which can function as national resources in the effort to remake the pattern of special education.

One idea fundamental to the successful evolution of special education is the "developmental model." This is not new, but it assumes crucial importance as a theoretical foundation for effective educational practice, both in the public schools and in residential settings. Wolf Wolfensberger has noted that the entire structure of organization and of service in residential facilities is based on the "medical model" (Kugel and Wolfensberger, 1969, pp. 68–70). If this is an inappropriate theoretical underpinning for residential programs, as suggested in the Alabama and Massachusetts court cases, it is all the more inapplicable in the context of special education. As Philip Roos (1970, 1971) has observed, there is certainly a significant role for the medical profession in the diagnosis and treatment of retarded and other handicapped children, but for the educator the "developmental model" is a more appropriate and more encouraging concept. He offers the following analysis (Roos, 1971, p. 23):

Mental retardation is not itself an illness. . . . Mental retardation can most fruitfully be handled as an impairment of the cognitive processes, and particularly of the capacity to learn. . . .

The relationship between professionals and retarded clients should be primarily structured in terms of a consulting, training or teaching relationship, in which the retarded is helped to cope more effectively with himself, with others, and with his physical environment. . . .

The Developmental Model suggests continuing evaluation of an individual's current level of functioning with on-going revision of program goals reflecting the present level of behavior. This model leads to a cycle of evaluation and programming, with maximum flexibility between program elements, so that clients can readily be shifted from program to program.

These comments about the mentally retarded apply with equal force to children with different handicapping conditions: deafness or impaired hearing, blindness or visual impairment, orthopedic disability, neurological dysfunction, emotional disturbance, and the myriad other deviant conditions that bring a child to the attention of the special educator.

Tannenbaum (1970) developed a theoretical model for a scientific and systematic approach to teaching; and Goldberg (1971a) adapted it for teaching the "trainable" and more severely retarded. In its basic principles, the model is equally applicable for retarded children at other degrees of handicap, and for students with different disabilities. Goldberg first raises the questions: "What is it we value? What ought we to be doing in the schools for trainable mentally retarded children?. . . Do we indeed value vocational training, development of personality, motivation, academic skills, relief to parents, social adjustment, sheer happiness, or use of leisure time?" He then presents a series of assumptions that underlie his model. Among them:

Special education is a process which helps the learner to change in many ways, some intentional, others quite unintentional.

If special education is a process which changes the learner, it is expected that each program, course, and unit of education will bring about some significant change or changes in the students.

The educational objectives or goals of instruction constitute the ways in which we would like to see the student change.

Parents . . . must be involved in the process of decision about educational goals and objectives.

On these assumptions, Goldberg presents the theoretical model, which includes the definition of several distinct roles for the teacher. It also incorporates specifics as to the *what* of instruction, the *how* of instruction, and the roles of communication input and output.

Personnel

An implication of the Pennsylvania "Right to Education" case that caused concern to knowledgeable people in the field, even those most enthusiastic for a favorable court decision, was the massive demand it would create for additional personnel. They had to be available within a matter of months, trained, willing, and ready to assume new responsibilities.

In Pennsylvania alone, the need would run into the thousands for teachers, teachers' aides, speech therapists, psychologists, and other professionals and paraprofessionals. Nationwide, the extension of the Pennsylvania principle could mean an instant doubling of the needed workers, and potentially quite a bit more, as standards were defined and imposed for special education.

A task that must be done proves do-able. The Pennsylvania Department of Education, faced with the task of identifying and evaluating thousands of children in a short time, in order to place them in appropriate educational programs by September 1972, managed to recruit some psychologists, to train others for the new specialized task, and to find and train teachers and the others needed to implement the court order.

Over a period of time, new sub-professions will evolve in response to the new tasks. The court called for "education and training appropriate to [the retarded child's] learning capacities." This was not likely to create a vast new demand for teachers of mathematics, geography, or foreign languages, but rather for a corps of sensitive human beings concerned and trainable for the tasks of special education in the classroom and in the home, where some of the newly discovered severely handicapped children might best receive the prescribed educational services.

There were sure to be new tasks for the special-education professionals in colleges of education, both in helping to define the new tasks and in training personnel to perform them. Quite likely, however, there would also be new responsibilities for the two-year community colleges, where the vocational or pre-professional training leading to an A.A. degree might well be appropriate to the new challenges of handicapped children heretofore excluded from school. Women already trained for nursery school, day care, and other pre-school programs for children of working mothers, could, with some additional training, become useful in the new classrooms. High school graduates and college students with summer recreation experience with the handicapped, and the parents of handicapped youngsters themselves, might well be recruited into the new fields of work in special education.

It required imagination, effort, and funds, but it could be done.

Joseph H. Douglass, executive director of the President's Committee on Mental Retardation, in a talk on "The Rights of the Retarded" early in 1972 at Glassboro State College, put the issue of personnel in a different focus: "Even if the state provides for the education of every child, and even if proper testing and placement procedures are followed, the welfare of the child ultimately rests with the teacher and her educational colleagues. This is particularly true with children from social, cultural, ethnic and economic backgrounds different from the so-called norm."

A social worker, writing in a medical journal (Adams, 1972), suggested the complexity of diagnosing and coping with deviant conditions in children:

With the rapid development of more sophisticated diagnostic procedures, we shall be confronted with an increasing number of precisely defined special handicaps that need ongoing regular medical care as well as specialist knowledge and skill. These handicaps will be embodied in individuals who live in families who are located in communities. In the past, medicine as a professional discipline combined its scientific clinical knowledge with social and sociologic insights, and the old-type community doctor coped with such problems as I have outlined in his stride, dealing with the pathologic index patient and the healthy nurturing family as a single entity. Today, the same situation and need prevail, and time and energy and emotional investment, even a seemingly disproportionate amount, must still be spent in helping the family of a retarded child to make the best social adaptation in this very disruptive event. If this vital aspect of medical practice is overlooked, sooner or later there will be negative repercussions—emotional, or social, or somatic in nature—of the same order that occur when a physical condition is not handled with maximum skill, insight and professional commitment.

Substitute *education* for "medical care" and *teachers* for "doctor," and the larger role of the professional in special education begins to take shape. It is not enough to minister to the deviant child's learning needs within the classroom; he is part of a family, in a community, and the educational system must address itself to the full social complex.

CHAPTER 10

Implications for Political and Social Action

"Right to Education" was important in its own right, and also because it was the first; but in the historical context it was merely a door opener. Other "Rights" quickly crowded in: the right to treatment, the right to habilitation.[1] The President's Committee on Mental Retardation, in its annual report *MR 71* (p. 17), listed among the "general rights of the mentally retarded":

The right to training
The right to medical treatment
The right to psychiatric treatment
The right to insurance
The right not to be experimented upon in institutions
The right not to be sterilized
The right to privacy
The right to marry

Not all of these rights have been affirmed by the courts, but they are, as the President's Committee said, receiving recognition and increasing acknowledgment. *New Directions,* the newsletter of the National Association of Coordinators of State Programs for the Mentally Retarded, reported in November 1971 that the attorneys general of the states of Maryland and Washington had issued rulings opening the way for mentally retarded citizens to exercise the right to vote.

---

[1]The Alabama and Massachusetts cases, almost simultaneous with that in Pennsylvania, extended the list of rights claimed. See above, pp. 51 ff.

There are differences that "make a difference" and differences that do not. This is one of the issues underlying the special-education questions of "zero reject" and of integration versus segregation. Segal (1972), a social worker, has noted that deviance is socially defined and that his professional colleagues have stereotyped deviants as incapable of influencing their own lives. He suggests that the definition of deviance is essentially a political act, and if this is so, there is a major role for advocates of the socially (or educationally) deviant.

In the past, judicial commitment procedures with respect to the mentally ill and the mentally retarded have often been perfunctory and without the semblance of genuine due process (Ross, 1959; Kay *et al.*, 1972, pp. 448–467, esp. p. 459). Persons suspected or accused of crimes, if they are identified as mentally retarded or diagnosed as "insane" for legal and judicial purposes, have at times been sent to state mental institutions, without fixed term, rather than standing trial and, if convicted, being sentenced to a correctional institution. There is serious question as to the validity of many such psychiatric decisions (Kutner, 1962; Allen *et al.*, 1968), but even if the accused persons were indeed found to be mentally ill or otherwise incompetent to stand trial, it seems their incompetence leads to a longer sentence, with less hope of rehabilitation, than if they were tried, convicted, and sentenced. This issue too is being tested in the courts as a matter of "rights of the retarded" in *Jackson v. Indiana.*

One implication of the rights of the handicapped is that, as a given facility is no longer suitable to their needs, they shall be able to move on to another, and in many cases a less restrictive, environment. If the residential facility for the mentally retarded in Alabama, Partlow State School and Hospital, is unable to fulfill the mandate placed on it by the court, the implication of the court order is that the residents shall be released and Partlow closed. But even if there is in fact the introduction of a genuine program of training and habilitation, enabling some of the residents at least to function at a higher level of competence and self-sufficiency, they have a right to expect that they may leave Partlow for a different way of life. A four-year experimental demonstration was undertaken by Elwyn Institute,[2] and the conclusion was: "It is possible to change a traditionally custodial institution into a rehabilitation facility, and to discharge a relatively large percentage of the educable retarded population to independent living."

Looking at the unmet—and to a considerable extent unexpressed

---

[2]The project and findings were summarized in a two-page *Research and Demonstration Brief*, published by the Social and Rehabilitation Service, U.S. Department of Health, Education, and Welfare, March 15, 1972. The full report, "A Transitional Program for Institutionalized Adult Retarded," has been published by the Elwyn Institute, Elwyn, Pennsylvania.

—needs of the mentally retarded, two thoughtful social workers have suggested that it may be necessary to develop a wholly new method of delivering services (Meenaghan and Mascari, 1971).

Providing varied services—schooling, vocational training, day care, recreation, and residential care—to mental retardates who need them and who have been denied them elsewhere has been the main objective that has led to the development of the field of mental retardation. . . . Whatever the many merits of the existing specialized services in the field, it is generally agreed that mental retardation agencies are not responding adequately to the volume of needs.

Meenaghan and Mascari then proceed to analyze the problem through another lens:

This failure [they say] is manifested in relation to two populations.

The first group involves those parents of retarded children who realize they need a service and apply for it. For this population waiting lists and long periods without service prevail because the demand for programs far exceeds the supply. However, the situation is even more disturbing for the second group—those who are currently neither receiving nor awaiting service from agencies. This is a sizable group.

They note a significant aspect of the mental retardation movement: that over the past twenty years and more, it has drawn much of its impetus and energy from "consumer" organization and involvement.[3] "What needs to be done now," they suggest, "is to heighten the somewhat latent consumer involvement in the philosophy and structure of the mental retardation agencies by broadening the base of the lay constituency and increasing lay responsibilities. Such an approach would attempt to maximize the coincidence between services and consumer-defined needs." To this end, they recommend a "new model," in which the salient features would be (1) a benefit system carried out with appropriate government intervention, and (2) a plan for consumer organization.

These two conditions would seem to describe exactly the circumstances currently developing out of the court decisions in Pennsylvania, Alabama, and elsewhere. Particularly with reference to education, but also to a considerable extent in the arena of residential services, the courts have ordered the appropriate agencies of government to provide services to all retarded persons in the prescribed categories. And effective implementation of the court orders will be speeded by organized parent action, such as was promptly evidenced by the Pennsylvania Association for Retarded Children.[4]

[3]See above, p. 10.
[4]See above, pp. 35, 39, 44.

Legislation

Legislatures acted before the 1971–72 round of "rights" cases in the courts,[5] and legislatures will continue to act and to react to social issues. Court decisions, widespread publicity, and political activism on the part of concerned parents and professionals, however, are three powerful influences impelling legislators to action. Thus, for a few significant examples, the California Legislature in 1970 enacted a measure specifying the level of performance on psychological tests required for placement in a class for the mentally retarded;[6] a bill was introduced in the New York Senate in 1972 to "phase out of existence the New York institutional state school system as it now exists";[7] a "Bill of Rights for the Mentally Retarded" was introduced into the United States Senate in June 1972;[8] and a member of Congress earlier in the year introduced two bills to guarantee a right to education for the mentally retarded.[9] None of these represents the last word; we can only be sure that there will be a great deal more legislative activity on issues such as these, at the state and Congressional levels.

Community Organization and Social Action

In the assertion, the testing, and the implementation of rights of handicapped children, there are roles for many participants: attorneys, legislatures, and courts, of course, but also parents and their organizations, teachers and other practitioners in special education, educational administrators, social workers, psychologists, researchers, and advocates.

None of this is new. The history of widening opportunities for handicapped children is the story of advocacy and social activism in its many forms (Katz, 1961; Segal, 1970; Lippman, 1970). What is relatively new is the enlistment of activist attorneys and the utilization of the courts as a mechanism.

Litigation is not a substitute for earlier modes of social action; it is simply one more channel for advocacy in behalf of the handicapped. The leadership of the Pennsylvania Association for Retarded Children recognized this from the start; attorney Gilhool emphasized the point in his first analysis of the problem,[10] and developments in

[5]See above, pp. 5 ff. and p. 11.

[6]Chapter 1569, Education Code.

[7]S. 10334. The bill did not pass.

[8]S. 3759; see above, p. 56.

[9]H.R. 12154 and H.R. 14033, both introduced by Congressman Charles A. Vanik (Ohio).

[10]See above, p. 20. See also Abeson, 1972a, p. 66.

Pennsylvania and elsewhere since the Federal court orders of 1971–72 have reinforced the recognition. All previous methods and channels must be utilized, along with the newest, if the mentally retarded are to receive their due.

The challenge to institutions (in the sociological sense) was a characteristic of the 1960's as it had not been since the era of national revolutions in the eighteenth century. Francis A. J. Ianni, anthropologist and professor of education at Teachers College, Columbia University, analyzed the development in a thoughtful essay:[11]

One by one the institutions of change are being attacked and challenged for their tendency to perpetuate status. Three years after students confronted Columbia University with charges of unresponsiveness to their needs and the needs of the community, the prisoners of Attica joined in an interracial demonstration rejecting a system designed to disable rather than rehabilitate the inmate. By these acts of rebellion the students and the inmates inadvertently began a process of education for themselves and their respective institutions—an education of involvement, relevance and change.

Those who challenge the system, demanding that they truly be educated or truly rehabilitated, have taken charge of their own lives and their own educations. In so doing, they discover within themselves the power to learn and to grow. They become their own educators. This liberating discovery, which is the kernel of true education, is precisely that which the institutions are so effective in obscuring. Such a discovery is a threat to the institution, unless the institution itself is engaged in a continuing process of growth and change. So far, the institutions have resisted change and, by virtue of their power, have apparently won the first battles. But the irony is clear to those who have joined the rebellion: the rebellion itself is the new institution.

Though I use the term "institution" loosely here, my use nevertheless points up my understanding of what institutions are: not fixed monolithic structures to be created and recast through clever manipulations of diagrams and organizational charts, but rather structured patterns of behavior which have grown out of social or individual needs as people work to fulfill them. In this sense, a rebellion is a model of an educational institution. It is faulty in many ways and costly, as the experience at Attica proved, but it is a dramatic model, clearly featuring involvement, relevance and growth. All are characteristics of an ideal educational institution. We can learn from this dramatization as we seek to facilitate, in an orderly and productive manner, the creation of viable educational institutions.

Less dramatic, but nevertheless powerful examples of alternative institutions, are apparent in such organizations as Synanon, Daytop, feminist organizations, and the Fortune Society. Although not usually thought of as educational institutions, fundamentally they are.

[11]"Alternatives for Community Education," *Perspectives on Education*, Teachers College, Winter-Spring 1972, pp. 16–23. The quotation is taken from p. 17.

What Ianni says of the institutions of the university and the penitentiary is at least equally true of the residential facility for the retarded and that other group of institutions, the special classes for exceptional children. What he says about feminist organizations and the Fortune Society is not literally true about handicapped children,[12] but it is true by analogy, for there are articulate spokesmen for the children in their parents, and potentially also their teachers and the "public interest" attorneys.

Dybwad (*The Exceptional Parent*, April–May 1972, p. 9) said: "Nothing very revolutionary is needed. For instance, a change to the effect that state governments have the same obligation to observe state laws, Federal laws, and state and Federal constitutions as everyone else." And Wolfensberger (1971, p. 35) predicted: "Consumers, in the new spirit of the consumer rights revolution, will file suit against such practices where they continue, and will win these suits." A scanning of newspaper reports published within a few months in 1972 disclosed many assertions of rights: of a high school student to wear long hair, of parents to see their children's school records, of children to visit their parents in jail, of a welfare recipient to receive a "fair hearing" before his payments were suspended, of an alleged "mad bomber" to gain release from a state mental hospital, of a girl to be a newspaper carrier. The courts are taking such suits seriously; apparently the civil rights cases of the 1960's and the mental retardation rights cases of the 1970's have awakened other oppressed minorities to assert their rights.

In an early comment on the Pennsylvania consent agreement and the interim court order of October 1971, the United Cerebral Palsy Associations observed that although the particular decision was specific for the retarded in Pennsylvania, it carried a message for all handicapped children in all the states.[13] "Parents in each state (including parents of cerebral palsied children) will have to take appropriate action in order to gain the right to an education for their children. In those states where cerebral palsied children are denied an education, UCP affiliates have an obligation to take such appropriate action." Under the heading "Strategy Alternatives," the national organization offered the following recommendations:

[12]In point of fact, the physically handicapped have begun to organize and to speak up for themselves. The *Washington Post* (May 6, 1972, p. B-2) reported: "Demonstrators in wheel chairs yesterday demanded equal rights for what they called the nation's largest minority: the disabled. More than 100 handicapped persons walked or were wheeled from the Washington Hilton—site of a President's Committee on Employment of the Handicapped meeting—to the Capitol." See also Patricia J. Thoben, "Disabled People March for Civil Rights," *Rehabilitation Record*, September–October 1972, pp. 24–26, and Susan Bliss, "The Mobilization of DIA," *Performance* (President's Committee on Employment of the Handicapped), May–June 1972, pp. 3–7. These were adults, but their demands implied assertion of the rights of handicapped children as well.

[13]Memorandum from Elsie D. Helsel, Washington Representative, March 10, 1972.

Although UCP is aware of, and sympathetic to, the problem of funding, personnel, and facilities that state departments of education as well as local and county school districts face in the light of this decision, our first responsibility is to our clients—individuals with cerebral palsy and their families.

Certainly the first step in trying to assure a free public education for all the cerebral palsied should be to contact the state officials responsible for special education and discuss strategies for achieving this goal within reasonable time limits.

Where state departments of education will not voluntarily undertake activities to insure the right to an education to all handicapped children in the state, there are three major alternatives available to affiliates and parents of cerebral palsied children.

1. If the state law permits an interpretation that mandates free education for the handicapped, a ruling can be sought from the Attorney General directing the State Department of Education to provide an appropriate educational experience for every child.

2. Where state school law, regulation or practice is discriminatory, affiliates and parents can file a complaint alleging the unconstitutionality of such laws under the Equal Protection Clause of the Fourteenth Amendment.

3. Where state laws are discriminatory, legislation can be introduced to remove the discriminatory provisions in the law.

And finally, UCP recommended:

Develop strategies in cooperation with other voluntary agencies serving the handicapped such as: Associations for Retarded Children, Councils for Exceptional Children, Easter Seal Societies, Epilepsy Foundation; and appropriate state agencies such as: Department of Education, Department of Welfare and Department of Mental Health/Mental Retardation.

It may be expected—and in the interest of the children, it is to be hoped—that organizations of parents of handicapped children will become increasingly active in this fashion.[14] What should also happen is the activation of teachers and others engaged in special education as a profession. By their choice of life work they have demonstrated a concern for handicapped children; and by their professional experience they have acquired knowledge that makes them truly expert in the world of laymen.

A professor of special education in the Pacific Northwest recently wrote: "The one area in which special educators' success throughout the years cannot be questioned, however, is public relations. Special

---

[14]Individual parents have long been anguished at the obstacles they find to fulfillment for their children. The most articulate among them have become leaders in the parent organizations. Relatively recently, they have begun to speak out. The June 1972 *Closer Look*, newsletter published by the Bureau of Education for the Handicapped, U.S. Department of Health, Education, and Welfare, contained vigorous communications from parents in several states, asking the right to participate in decisions affecting their children.

education has successfully taught both the general public and the field of education to recognize and deal with exceptional children" (Lilly, 1971, p. 747). This assertion seems hard to substantiate, as we contemplate the state of public and professional acceptance of special education as of the date of publication. What is not in doubt, however, is the fact that special educators will indeed have to become proficient in what Lilly calls "public relations," but which we prefer to think of as enlightened public awareness of the special needs of exceptional children.

The energetic efforts of the National Association for Retarded Children, United Cerebral Palsy Associations, the President's Committee on Mental Retardation, the Advertising Council, and associated organizations made their impact in the 1950's and 1960's, but there is much yet to be done in the reshaping of public attitudes toward the handicapped (Lippman, 1972, Chapter 11). Indeed, the public-informational success of the two decades past is attributable more to the energy, skill, and sheer volume of effort of parents of handicapped children than to any conscious achievement of the special educators as a profession. Perhaps now—with the added impetus of court decisions—if the educators will add their weight to that of the parents and other interested citizens, it will be possible to extend the accomplishments that began with voluntary organizations and legislative enactments.

Now (meaning 1973, 1974 . . . 1980) is the time of decision. Courts, legislatures, administrative officials in the executive branch of state government, county commissioners, municipal officials, local boards of education and school superintendents, individual principals are making decisions that will have the effect of including or excluding handicapped children from the mainstream. In education, in recreation, in work training and employment opportunity, in all aspects of community acceptance that can mean the full, satisfying life for each handicapped individual, the decisions are being made now.

Each of those decisions is made within a framework of laws, regulations, procedural routines, and (often unspoken) assumptions. It is in these arenas that the friends of handicapped children (and adults) can influence the decisions.

The parents, the teachers, the social workers, and the lawyers, working together, can capitalize on the momentum generated by the Pennsylvania and other court decisions of the early 1970's. They can do so by continuing to seek enforcement of their children's rights through the courts; but they must also continue to use the levers that have proved so useful in the past: legislative advocacy, political action, pressure upon public officials at every level, organizational efforts in behalf of the *whole* class of handicapped children, and, accompanying all other efforts, the many uses of publicity.

The new involvement of the courts has been spelled out in this publication, and the value of this protector of human rights is clear. Less obvious is the role of the "public interest" lawyer. He is a new phenomenon: the attorney of the stripe of Tom Gilhool, and his counterparts of the Alabama, District of Columbia, and similar cases. These young counselors received their formal training in some of the most respected law schools in the country. They had the opportunity to join the most prestigious law firms, and some of them did so. A few of them, however—and an increasing number—found corporate law stultifying, and the prospect of rising income and status boring. Some, including some of the brightest, broke away.[15] They joined the staffs of Legal Aid Societies, they became volunteers for the American Civil Liberties Union, they went on government payrolls to help poor people bring suits against Federal and state governments, they took up the issues of civil rights and welfare rights and tenants' rights—and they have begun to work for the retarded and other handicapped children (Lubenow, 1972).

Advocacy

Eleanor Elkin, past president of the National Association for Retarded Children, raised some questions in a statement to the Department of Health, Education, and Welfare in connection with its inquiry on Willowbrook State School (*Mental Retardation News,* May 1972). Why, she asked, are there so many institutions in the United States that appear to be competing for recognition as "next to worst" in the nation? "It is not because we have not taken stands," she said. "It is not because we do not have the knowledge. It is not that funds can't be found." The "stumbling blocks to change," she suggested, were:

Parents, who fear possible retaliation against their child if they speak too loudly; parents who fear their child in the institution may be forgotten as attention is drawn to community residential programs . . .

Bureaucracy, with its power struggles and empire building. Bureaucracy, whose members must nervously defend their jobs and their territory . . .

Civil Service regulations that protect incompetents and rigidly prevent the hiring of some desirable candidates; a reluctance to abandon outdated philosophies; and

Public belief in the necessity of mass care for retarded persons.

[15]"New Breed of Lawyer: Jersey a Center for Legal Activists," *Newark Star-Ledger,* May 28, 1972, p. 1; "2,200 O.E.O. Lawyers Who Provide Free Counseling to the Poor Finding Satisfaction in Their Work," *New York Times,* July 6, 1972, p. 17.

The answer, Mrs. Elkin said, would be an Advocacy Agency, separate from the deliverer of service, to break through the bureaucratic immobility to meet the needs and protect the rights of the individual. Joseph T. Weingold, long-time executive director of the New York State Association for Retarded Children, likewise talks of advocacy. In a 12-page narrative memorandum,[16] he proposed the creation of an "apparatus" that would delineate the legal rights of the retarded; serve as a receiving center for the needs of the retarded, with outreach responsibilities to the community; and serve as an adversary advocate for the handicapped child, "in and out of institutions, vis-à-vis the community agency or the state itself."

The role of the advocate has been essayed in various forms around the world. The most comprehensive, perhaps, is the Ombudsman role, as exercised in Denmark and in Sweden. In California, the Regional Centers were designed as lifelong agencies of service to the mentally retarded, and by later amendment they have assumed the role of guardians at the request of parents (Dinkelspiel, 1969; Kay *et al.*, 1972). Nebraska has developed a specific Citizens Advocate Program, drawing on the formulations of Wolf Wolfensberger and working through the Capitol Association for Retarded Children. J. Iverson Riddle, superintendent of Western Carolina Center, tried a variant at the North Carolina residential facility.

None of these, at least in the United States, seems fully effective at this time. Pending the establishment of a more formal and comprehensive advocate agency,[17] the role continues to devolve upon the parents of the handicapped and those professional workers with a genuine concern beyond the call of duty.

In a proposal for an "ombudsman for the retarded," Payne (1970) suggested that such an official would have a useful role in a residential setting for retarded persons, in the public schools, in vocational rehabilitation offices, and in a community agency, such as the office of the local health and welfare council. "To the extent that retarded children are arbitrarily admitted to or dismissed from special education classes in public schools," he wrote, "there is a need for an ombudsman there. An ombudsman in the schools could further help to assure that the children in the special education program receive the full measure of their entitlement under law, that their general and special rights were protected, and that educational opportunities commensurate with their abilities were fully and continuously

[16]"Description of an Advocacy System to Protect the Rights of the Mentally Retarded," March 1972.

[17]In an address in connection with the 1970 White House Conference on Children, Senator Walter F. Mondale (Minnesota) proposed an "advocate for children" (*Congressional Record*, December 9, 1970), but the idea has not moved toward enactment.

available to them."[18] Later, from a somewhat different perspective, Payne (1972) wrote:

Several generic elements of ombudsmanship have implications for social work curricula. One is the importance of law and policy. In any setting the ombudsman's function includes assuring the just and fair administration of relevant laws and policies that vary according to the area of work. Thus any educational program for would-be ombudsmen should stress (1) appreciation of the legal foundation's importance in any program or service and (2) practice in interpreting basic law and policy in relation to specific problem cases. These topics may not now be included in the curricula of social work schools but should be if a significant number of social workers begin to function as ombudsmen. Closely related to appreciation of the law's importance and practice in relating law and policy to specific cases, is the ombudsman's need to understand thoroughly bureaucratic structure and organization. If an ombudsman intends to improve a bureaucratic system's service and decisions, he must understand not only the system but also the general theory of administration and bureaucratic organization.

There are two points to be made on the basis of this series of observations. One is that, with such an orientation, social workers as a professional group can be a useful ally of the retarded and their families. The other is that the same injunctions Payne makes about schools of social work apply with equal force to colleges of education.

Advocacy in a formal, legalistic sense must remain the function of a public agency (as in the Scandinavian Ombudsman) or in the voluntary sector the organization of parents of the handicapped. Less formally, it is a role that can be assumed by anyone who cares. The "public interest" lawyers have already shown their concern, and they continue to be available. They need, as partners, the families of the handicapped, the teachers, and all the others who work with exceptional children.

---

[18]Although this was written before the Pennsylvania case was filed, and in the one state at least the court has now entered as an ally, the point seems to be still valid that an independent official with ombudsman-like responsibilities and authority would help assure the rights of the retarded.

APPENDIX A

Cases in Point

Adams v. Lucy, 351 U.S. 931, 76 S. Ct. 790, 700 L. ed. 1480 (1956)

Bolling v. Sharpe, 347 U.S. 497, 74 S. Ct. 693, 98 L. ed. 884 (1954)

Brown v. Board of Education, 347 U.S. 483, 74 S. Ct. 686, 98 L. Ed. 873 (1954)

Brown v. Board of Education, 349 U.S. 294, 75 S. Ct. 753, 99 L. Ed. 1083 (1955)

Bush v. Orleans Parish School Board, 190 F. Supp. 861 (E.D. La., 1960)

Byrd v. McCready, 340 U.S. 827 (1950)

Cooper v. Aaron, 358 U.S. 1, 78 S. Ct. 1401, 3 L. Ed. 2d 5 (1958)

Covarrubias v. San Diego Unified School District, 70–394 Texas Reports (February 1971)

Diana v. State Board of Education, C–70 37 RFP, District Court for Northern California (February 1970)

Florida ex rel. Hawkins v. Board of Control, 350 U.S. 413, 76 S. Ct. 693, 100 L. Ed. 486 (1956)

Griffin v. County School Board of Prince Edward County, 377 U.S. 218, 84 S. Ct. 1226, 12 L. Ed. 256 (1964)

Hobson v. Hansen, 393 U.S. 801, 89 S. Ct. 40, 21 L. Ed. 2d 85 (1968)

Jackson v. Indiana, 39 Law Week 3413; 40 Law Week 3247

Mills et al. v. Board of Education of the District of Columbia et al., District of Columbia, Civil Action No. 1939–71

Missouri ex rel. Gaines v. Canada, 305 U.S. 337, 59 S. Ct. 232, 83 L. Ed. 208 (1938)

Pennsylvania Association for Retarded Children, Nancy Beth Bowman et al. v. Commonwealth of Pennsylvania, David H. Kurtzman et al., E. D. Pa., Civil Action No. 71–42 (1972), 334 F. Supp. 1253 (1971)

Ricci et al. v. Greenblatt et al., M. D. Mass., Civil Action No. 72–469F (1972)

Robinson et al. v. Cahill et al., 118 N.J. Super. 223 (1972)

Rodriguez v. San Antonio, 337 F. Supp. 280 (W.D. Texas, 1971)

Serrano v. Priest, 5 Cal. 3d 584, 487 P. 2d 1241 (1971)

Sipuel v. Board of Regents, 332 U.S. 631, 68 S. Ct. 299, 92 L. Ed. 247 (1948)

Spangler v. Pasadena City Board of Education, 311 F. Supp. 501 (C.D. Cal., 1970)

Stewart v. Phillips, C.A. No. 70–1199–F (D. Mass., 1971)

Sweatt v. Painter, 339 U.S. 629, 71 S. Ct. 13, 94 L. Ed. 1114 (1950)

Van Dusartz v. Hatfield, 334 F. Supp. 870 (D. Minn., 3d Div., 1971)

Wisconsin v. Constantineau, 397 U.S. 985, 90 S. Ct. 1125, 25 L. Ed. 2nd 393 (1970)

Wyatt v. Stickney et al., M.D. Ala., Civil Action No. 3185-N (1972)

Numerous related cases are cited in the plaintiffs' memorandum in support of the motion for a three-judge court, prepared by Thomas K. Gilhool, attorney for the plaintiffs, and in the court's final opinion of May 5, 1972 (see Appendix D). *Brown v. Board of Education* and other civil rights cases dealing with discrimination and segregation in public education are summarized in Berger (1967), especially pp. 133–142. Cases involving testing and special education placement are described in Ross *et al.* (1971).

Basic Commitments and Responsibilities to Exceptional Children

A Position paper adopted by the Council for Exceptional Children at its Miami Convention in April, 1971; prepared by the CEC Policies Commission.

Willard Abraham	John Johnson
Donald Blodgett	Fred MacKinnon
Frances Connor	Paul Voelker

Maynard Reynolds, Chairman

Education is the right of all children.

The principle of education for all is based on the philosophical premise of democracy that every person is valuable in his own right and should be afforded equal opportunities to develop his full potential. Thus, no democratic society should deny educational opportunities to any child, regardless of his potentialities for making a contribution to society. Since the passage of the first public-school laws in the mid-nineteenth century, the principle has received general endorsement and qualified execution. While lip service has been paid to the intent of the principle, various interpretations of the terms "education" and "all children" have deprived many children of their right.

The ordinary educational opportunities provided by the schools have tended to neglect or exclude children with unusual learning needs: the gifted; the physically, mentally, and emotionally handicapped; and the victims of socioeconomic and cultural differences.

These children need special education—specialized diagnostic and instructional services—and, in order to be able to benefit fully from the education, they need the opportunity to view themselves as acceptable to society. They need stable and supportive home lives, wholesome community interactions, and the opportunity to view themselves and others in a healthy manner.

Because of their exceptionality, many of the children need to begin their school experiences at earlier ages than are customary for children in our society, many need formal educational services well into adulthood, and many require health and social services that are closely coordinated with school programs. Meeting these needs is essential to the total development of exceptional children as individuals and as members of society.

For some decades now, educators and schools have been responding to the challenge of educating the exceptional children. At least five times as many school systems provide special educational services today as a quarter of a century ago. Still, not all children are being provided for fully; relatively few services exist for the intellectually gifted child, for example, and less than half of the children who need highly specialized services are receiving them. The community should extend its demand that school personnel must learn to understand and serve the individual needs of these children as well as those more easily accommodated in the educational system. The surge of interest among educators in individualizing instruction hopefully will mean more sensitivity to the educational needs of all children, and particularly to those with special needs.

The problem of providing special educational services is admittedly multiple and complex. Many interest groups, such as the parents of handicapped, inner-city, minority-group children, and community organizations, and the frequent legislative studies at both state and national levels, have created many issues over the direction and kinds of services that should be provided. Who should be educated? What are the rights of the family in determining the education of exceptional children? What is the role of the school and other agencies in providing services for the exceptional child and his family? These issues must be resolved if the right of education for all is to be reflected in a meaningful commitment to and provision of education for every child.

The policies proposed here are an attempt to clarify the basic commitments and responsibilities of Special Educators, those educators whose professional competencies center on educating exceptional children. This position paper[1] is the first in a series initiated

---

[1]Developed in a series of discussions from an original draft statement by Maynard C. Reynolds and Coralie Wells Dietrich.

by a new Policies Commission of the Council for Exceptional Children; it is the hope of the Council that the position papers will become a seminal force for continuing change. Each policy statement is preceded by a discussion that establishes the rationale for the statement. In order to keep the paper within a reasonable size limit, the discussions are necessarily kept to a minimum.

While the statement which follows pertains mainly to handicapped children the Policies Commission plans an early position paper dealing with the issues of educating gifted children.

I. The Goal and Commitment of Special Education

The fundamental purposes of Special Education are the same as those of regular education: the optimal development of the individual as a skillful, free, and purposeful person, able to plan and manage his own life and to reach his highest potential as an individual and as a member of society. Indeed, Special Education developed as a set of highly specialized areas of education in order to provide exceptional children with the same opportunities as other children for a meaningful, purposeful, and fulfilling life.

To Special Educators, the statements of educational goals that stress the primacy of intellectual development are inadequate. They have learned from their experiences with children who have learning problems that so-called "intelligent" behavior is interrelated with individual motivation, cultural values, physical competency, self-esteem, and other non-cognitive variables.

Perhaps the most important concept that has been developed in Special Education as the result of experiences with exceptional children, is that of the fundamental individualism of every child. The aspiration of Special Educators is to see every child as a unique composite of potentials, abilities, and learning needs for whom an educational program must be designed to meet his particular needs. From its beginnings, Special Education has championed the cause of children with learning problems. It is as the advocates of such children and of the concept of individualization that Special Education can come to play a major creative role in the mainstream of education.

The special competencies of Special Educators are more than a collection of techniques and skills. They comprise a body of knowledge, methods, and philosophical tenets that are the earmark of the professions. As professionals, Special Educators are dedicated to the optimal education of exceptional children and they reject the misconception of schooling that is nothing but custodial care.

Policy:

The focus of all education should be the unique learning needs of the individual child, and of the child as a total functioning organism. All educators should recognize and accept the identity of fundamental purposes in both special and regular education.

The purpose of special education is to enlarge the variety of educational programs for all children so that the individualization of programs may be furthered as a way of fulfilling the fundamental purposes of education for all children, whatever their needs.

As advocates of the rights of all children to education, special educators affirm their professionalism.

II. Implementation of Universal Education

A. Compulsory Services and Compulsory Attendance

The provision of universal education for children in a democratic society has been translated as a commitment to the providing of educational opportunities for every child, whatever may be his socio-economic status; cultural or racial origins; physical, intellectual, or emotional equipment; potential contribution to society; and whatever his educational needs may be. This commitment to *every child* thus includes a commitment to children with unusual learning needs and to those with outstanding abilities and talents. Although providing education for these children may require a variety of specialized services and instructional programs, some costly and some requiring radical innovations in traditional educational structures, there is no test that can be used to include some children and exclude others where the principle of universal education is concerned.

Some of the specialized services that may be essential if exceptional children are to attend school include the provision of transportation facilities, functional architectural environments, personalized equipment aids, individualized instruction programs, and special education and supporting personnel. Certainly the dollar-and-cents outlay for such programs may be great; if they are not instituted and maintained, however, the cost of neglect is infinitely greater and must be borne mainly by the children as well as by their families, the communities, and society as a whole.

Policy:

The concept of universal education includes exceptional children as well as others. Efforts should be strongly supported to make explicit the obligations of local and state and provincial governments to educate exceptional children.

State and provincial requirements concerning education should include participation in educational programs by all exceptional children.

B. *Early and Continuing Education*

Schools have traditionally assumed educational responsibilities for children beginning at about age five or six years and ending with late adolescence. Increasingly, it is apparent that formal educational experiences at earlier ages would pay rich dividends in the full development of the capabilities of many exceptional children. Special Educators now have much useful knowledge and technique for working with very young exceptional children. What is needed is the identification of the children who could benefit from early education and the actual implementation of programs.

Communities should make their schools responsible for conducting search and census operations through which children who may need specialized education at very early ages can be identified. The voluntary enrollment of such children by their parents is inadequate because many parents may not be aware of the child's special needs or of available forms of assistance. An important part of early education programs are procedures for child study that encourage adaptations to the particular needs of very young exceptional children.

Individuals with special talents, gifts, or handicaps frequently need education and periodic re-education beyond the traditional school-leaving ages. To encourage the continuing development of youths and adults and to maximize their contributions to society vigorous efforts are necessary to provide them with vocational education, placement services, employment counseling, and job training. For any child with educational problems, the schools should provide the facilities for the continuation of his education or for retraining when necessary at whatever age.

Policy:

Schools should provide educational services for individuals according to their needs and regardless of age.

Schools should actively seek out children who may have specialized educational needs in the first years of their lives. A particular commitment should be made to initiate home-care training programs for parents of infants with special needs, to establish specialized nursery-school and kindergarten programs, and to utilize specialized components of regular early education programs to serve exceptional children.

Competency and maximal development should be the criteria for terminating an individual's schooling rather than age. Ideally, no person's formal education would ever be terminated; the school should always be ready to serve his educational and training needs as required for his optimal development as an independent, productive person.

C. The Maintenance of Attendance:
School Excuse, Exclusion, and Expulsion

The schools' commitment to compulsory, universal education has often been circumvented by the indiscriminate use of excuse, exclusion, and expulsion. Children with problems have frequently been demitted from schools on the dubious grounds that they were uneducable, had undesirable characteristics, or disrupted the education of other children.

A host of legal decisions in recent years has emphasized the right of children to attend school unless their presence is provably harmful to others. Other decisions have enunciated the doctrine that children have a legal right to education and, therefore, cannot be excluded from all or part of school activities without legal procedures.

When a child is suspended from all or part of the school activities as a disciplinary measure, the suspension should be for a limited period, the order should include provisions for the child's re-entry, and the date of re-entry should be definite.

Although children are normally excused from school for routine reasons of illness or family arrangements, long-term excuses should be permitted only under extraordinary conditions and under continual review.

Since no child's right to education may be legally abrogated, the exclusion of any child on the ground that no facilities are available for him cannot be tolerated. For the past three decades the trend in state and provincial laws has been to develop special education services at local levels; the special programs for a small number of exceptional children that may seem impractical can often be made possible by innovative approaches and uses of available regular and consultative personnel.

Policy:
The excuse, exclusion, or expulsion of children from all or part of school activities should not be permitted except under extraordinary conditions with due acknowledgement of the children's legal rights.

1. All demissions should be for stated periods of time and should include definite provisions for admitting or re-admitting the children to school.

2. Children so demitted should remain the continuing responsibilities of the schools: their demissions should be under continuous review so that the children can be re-admitted as soon as possible.

3. Outside agencies should be involved when necessary to facilitate the children's re-admission.

4. An accurate register should be maintained by local school agencies and by state or provincial agencies of all children excused, excluded, or expelled from all or parts of school programs and of the reasons for the demissions.

These agencies should concern themselves with solving problems attendant to the demissions.

5. To prevent the exclusion of exceptional children from local schools, state and provincial agencies should assess the gaps and needs in communi-ty services and cooperate with the local schools in filling them.

III. Special Education Within the Schools

A. *The Relations of Special and Regular School Programs*

Special Education is an integral part of the total educational enter-prise, not a separate order. In any school system Special Education is a means of enlarging the capacity of the system to serve the educa-tional needs of all children.

The particular function of Special Education within the schools (and the education departments of other institutions) is to identify children with unusual needs and to aid in the effective fulfillment of those needs. This fulfillment, at the present time, is accomplished in many regular school programs as well as by many special programs that cannot be included in regular classrooms by teachers without assistance. A primary goal of educators should be to help build accommodative learning opportunities for exceptional children in mainstream educational programs. In the implementation of this goal Special Education can serve as a support system; Special Edu-cators can assist regular school personnel in managing the education of exceptional children.

When the special placement of a child is required, the aim of the placement should be to maximize the development and freedom of the child rather than to accommodate the regular classroom.

Policy:

Special education should function within and as a part of the regular, public-school framework. Within this framework, the function of special education should be to participate in the creation and maintenance of a total educational environment suitable for all children.

From their base in the regular school system special educators can foster the development of specialized resources by coordinating their specialized contributions with the contributions of the regular school system. One of the primary goals of special educators should be the enhancement of regular school programs as a resource for all children.

B. *The Placement of Children in Special School Programs*

Special Education takes many forms and can be provided within a broad spectrum of administrative arrangements. Agreement is general that children with special educational needs should be served in regular classrooms and neighborhood schools insofar as these arrangements are conducive to good educational progress. It is necessary sometimes, however, to provide special supplementary services for exceptional children or to remove them from parts or all of regular programs. Sometimes it is even necessary to remove some children from their homes and communities for placement in residential schools, hospitals, or training centers. Even when residential school placements have been made, it is desirable that the children attend local community schools for parts of their schooling. Under such programs, it is essential that the local schools be fully willing to accept the children.

The continuum from regular to highly specialized schools (often residential) represents the broad range of educational programs that is available to meet the individual needs of exceptional children. It is not uncommon for children to be placed into one or another Special Education facility by processes of rejection or by simplistic testing-categorizing methods rather than by careful decisions that seek to optimize the benefits for the children. When no options exist, as often occurs in the planning for gifted children or those with severe handicaps, and when decisions are made poorly, the children are denied their fundamental rights to free, public education and the education authorities violate the basic tenets of our democratic society.

Schools as a whole and in all their parts are a resource for children and placements should be made among and within them only for valid educational reasons. In the process the psycho-social needs of the children should not be overlooked. Like all children, exceptional children need environmental stability, emotional nurturance and social acceptance.

Policy:
Special education should be arranged for exceptional children whenever feasible to protect the stability of their home, school, and community relationships and to enhance their self-concepts. Special Education placements, particularly those involving separation from community, school and home life, should be made only after careful study and for compelling reasons.

Within schools the placement of all children should maximize their opportunities for the best possible education. Specialized placements that are effected crudely and simply by the rejection of children from regular school situations are educationally and morally indefensible. Special education is not and should not be used as a residual operation or catchall for children who are difficult to teach. Equally indefensible is the failure to develop needed differentiation of school programs that results in the confinement of pupils in inappropriate educational settings.

C. Elimination of the Labeling-Categorizing of Children

The field of Special Education is concerned with children who have unusual needs and with school programs that employ unusual techniques. As the result of early attitudes and programs that stressed assistance for severely handicapped children, the field developed a vocabulary and practices based on the labeling and categorizing of children. In recent decades the labeling-categorizing was extended to children with milder degrees of exceptionality. The continued use of the terms, unfortunately, tends to rigidify the thinking of all educators on the significance and purposes of Special Education and to be dysfunctional and even harmful for the children.

Words such as "defective," "disabled," "retarded," "impaired," "disturbed," and "disordered," when attached to children with special needs, are stigmatic labels that produce unfortunate results in both the children and the community's attitudes toward the children. The problems are magnified when the field organizes and regulates its programs around classification systems that define categories of children according to such terms. Many of the classifications are oriented to etiology, prognosis, or necessary medical treatment rather than to educational classifications, and are of little value to the schools. Simple psychometric thresholds, which have sometimes been allowed to become pivotal considerations in educational decision making, present another set of labeling problems.

The most valuable contribution to education that Special Education makes is in terms of its specialized knowledge and competencies, values, and procedures for individualizing educational programs for individual children, whatever their special needs. Indeed, Special Educators at their most creative are the advocates of children who are not well-served by schools except by special arrangements. To further the understanding and servicing of such children, Special Educators as well as other educational personnel should eliminate the use of simplistic categorizing.

No one can deny the importance of some of the variables that traditionally have had importance in Special Education such as intelligence, hearing, and vision. However, these variables in all their complex forms and degrees must be assessed in terms of educational relevance for a particular child. Turning the variables into typologies that may contribute to excesses in labeling-categorizing children is indefensible and should be eliminated.

In the past many legislative and regulating systems have specified criteria for including children in an approved category as the starting point for specialized programming and funding. The practice places high incentives on the labeling of children and undoubtedly results in the erroneous placement of many children. It is desirable that financial aids be tied to educational programs rather than to children and that systems for allocating children to specialized programs be much more open than in the past.

Policy:
Special Educators should enhance the accommodative capacity of schools and other educational agencies to serve children with special needs more effectively. In identifying such children, Special Educators should be concerned with the identification of their educational needs, not with generalized labeling or categorizing of children.

Decisions about the education of children should be made in terms of carefully individualized procedures that are explicitly oriented to the children's developmental needs.

To further discourage the labeling-categorizing of children, programs should be created on the basis of the educational functions served rather than on the basis of categories of children served.

Regulatory systems that enforce the rigid categorization of pupils as a way of allocating them to specialized programs are indefensible. Financial aids for Special Education should be tied to specialized programs rather than to finding and placing children in those categories and programs.

D. *The Need for Flexibility and Development*

Because of rapid changes and developments in the environmental factors that influence the characteristics of children and the conditions of their lives, Special Education should maintain a flexibility that permits it to adapt to changing requirements.

Some of the events and changes that have had major impact on Special Education in recent years are the following: a rubella epidemic, discovery of preventatives for retrolental fibroplasia, increasing number of premature births, increasing awareness of the deleterious effects of poverty and malnutrition, new techniques in surgical intervention, invention of individual electronic hearing aids, and adaptation of low-vision aids. Changes and developments in public health, medicine, technology, and social programs may have only a small total effect in school systems but they frequently have major impacts on Special Education programs. Changes in one aspect of Special Education quickly are reflected in other aspects of the field as, for example, the rapid development of day-school programs for exceptional children which has been reflected by a more severely handicapped population in residential schools.

Policy:

Special Educators must seek to be highly flexible in the provision of services and the use of technology and techniques to meet the changing needs of exceptional children.

School administrators and Special Educators have particular responsibility for sustaining their professional awareness and development as a basis for changing programs to meet changing needs.

E. The School and Comprehensive Services

Over the decades schools have increasingly broadened their services to children and communities in many ways as, for example, adding school psychologists and social workers to the regular staffs. There is a growing movement among educators to become general child advocates and to make the school a broad developmentally-oriented, competency-producing agency that takes over functions sometimes assigned to other agencies. By contrast, strong voices are also urging that schools limit their activities. They want schools to restrict their concerns to raising the intellectual levels of children and to avoid substituting themselves for other agencies or placing themselves *in loco parentis.*

At issue is the question of what role schools and other agencies should play in meeting the needs of exceptional children and in responding to the demands for a wide range of services from the families of such children. At the root of the issue is the problem that many children and their families need coordinated services in health, recreation, and welfare, as well as in education. The achievement of coordinated child-centered and family-centered services is difficult because of the fragmentation of responsibilities for those services among many agencies and professions. The school's role in the development of comprehensive programs is in a state of confusion because of the differing points of view.

The Educational Policies Commission, a former joint venture of the National Education Association and the American Association of School Administrators, issued two statements on the problem, a decade apart in time, each embracing a different point of view. The 1939 statement, entitled *Social Services and the Schools,* advocated the limited view that health, welfare, and recreation services should function outside the schools and meet the schools' concerns through liaison and persuasion. This arrangement can be criticized on the grounds of its looseness and diffusion of leadership, authority, and responsibility.

The 1948 statement, *Education for All American Children,* proposed that schools provide the children of a community with a broad range of services including, among others, health, psychological, welfare, and family counseling services; residential programs for exceptional children from rural areas; nursery school and early education programs in the home; and provisions for dropouts based on concern for the problems of minority groups.

No clear answers can be proposed here. The issue indicates, however, that very real problems about the role of schools exist and that solutions must be sought.

Policy:
As long as exceptional children need comprehensive services, schools should be actively concerned with the problem of *how* such services can be best provided. Because the availability of comprehensive services is related to the purposes of education for exceptional children, schools should be prepared to go beyond their traditional role as coordinators or users of other community services and lead the way in developing new and experimental forms of comprehensive child and family services.

IV. The School and the Family

The family is the fundamental social unit in our culture. As such it is invested with primary rights and obligations regarding the education of the child. The parents must have access to all available necessary information in order to be able to make optimal decisions about the child's education and to fulfill the family's obligations to the child. In recognition of these rights and because wholesome family relationships are vital requisites to the child's educational development, the school should establish mechanisms to provide adequate counseling and family services to insure that the parental participation in the decision-making processes will be on an informed basis. More broadly, the school should establish whatever structures are needed to create a genuine partnership with parents and community organizations in designing and implementing educational programs.

One of the most significant and promising developments in our society is the steady extension of participation in policy making to consumers of services. It is healthy and desirable that parents and lay groups should make their particular concerns known and have a part in policy formation. The consumers of services—the children themselves—are a valuable resource in evaluating the organization and delivery of services; they should not be ignored.

The child is not only a family member but an individual with basic rights to total educational development. When his basic rights as an individual and citizen are violated, even unwittingly and without malevolent intent on the part of the family, the school as an agent of the state should assume the necessary responsibilities to assure the child's rights to the fullest development of his capacities. It is urgently important that the schools employ qualified personnel to perform in this domain as it is an extremely sensitive area.

Policy:

As a means of strengthening Special Education programs, the parents of exceptional children and organized community groups should be given a responsible voice in educational policy formation and planning activities.

The primary consumers of educational services, the children, should not be ignored as a valuable resource in the evaluation of the organization and delivery of services.

As a means of strengthening the family in fulfilling its obligations to children with exceptional needs, the schools should provide educationally-related counseling and family services. In cases of clear educational neglect, the schools, through qualified professional personnel, should make extraordinary arrangements for educational services.

V. The Responsibility of Higher Education

Historically, the training programs for teachers and other educational personnel needed to operate Special Education Programs were started in service centers such as institutions for blind, deaf, and retarded children. Subsequently, a few colleges launched summer training programs in the early 1900's; by the 1930's, full-fledged programs were functioning in perhaps half a dozen colleges in the United States.

Only after World War II did large numbers of colleges and universities become involved in full sequences of special education training and, even into the 1970's many regions are left unserved by higher education. Even shorter is the history of research activities in Special Education as aspects of higher education functions.

Although programs for exceptional children can be and often have been started without specialized personnel, the training resources of colleges and universities are needed in support of quality programs. Through their full participation, training programs can be instituted that are creatively oriented and field related; and inservice training programs to upgrade and expand the expertise of personnel already working in the area can be established.

Policy:

Colleges and universities have an obvious but, at this time, not completely filled obligation to develop and coordinate their resources in support of programs for exceptional children. The obligation comprises a number of factors:

1. to provide through scholarly inquiry an expanded knowledge base for Special Education programs;
2. to provide training for various professional and paraprofessional personnel needed to conduct programs for handicapped and gifted children;
3. to cooperate in the development and field testing of innovative programs;
4. to provide for the coordinated development of programs across disciplines and professions so that training and service models are congruent with emerging models for comprehensive community services;
5. to provide all students, whether or not they are in programs relating specifically to handicapped and gifted children, a basis for understanding and appreciating human differences;
6. to exemplify in their own programs of training, research, and community service—and even in their architecture—a concern for accommodating and upgrading the welfare of handicapped and gifted persons;
7. to cooperate with schools, agencies, and community groups in the creation and maintenance of needed Special Education programs.

VI. Levels of Government Responsibility for the Support of Special Education

An important set of policy questions for the organization and delivery of special educational services is concerned with the allocation of public responsibilities at the different governmental levels: local and intermediate,[2] state and provincial, and federal. One of the basic tenets of a democratic society is that education should be free, universal, equal, and designed to further each individual's optimal development. In implementing these principles, the different governments must provide not only financial supports, but legal, political and administrative assistance as well. The intent and provision of laws relating to education must be translated into action at every governmental level.

Since education is not a static process, the governmental agencies responsible for carrying out the legal mandates must provide leadership at every level to encourage improvement and innovation in the schools.

[2]The term "intermediate" refers to special consortiums of local districts or to broad regional or zonal organizations that carry responsibility for specialized services within a broader than local-district school area.

Local School Districts

Policy:

Local and intermediate school districts should provide continuing support for their educational services, including participation in the financing of every educational program in the locality.

The local or primary school district should be responsible for conducting at least annual reviews of all children who are legal residents of the district (although they may be placed outside the district) to assure that the education of each child is proceeding adequately. The school district should maintain a completely up-to-date roster of all its children and excuse, expell, or exclude children from school only under extraordinary conditions.

The district carries major responsibility for the quality of its Special Education programs and for coordination with other agencies to achieve comprehensive child-centered services.

State and Provincial Governments

Policy:

The basic responsibility for providing educational programs for all children rests with state and provincial governments. They should provide financial supports to develop and encourage the improvement of comprehensive educational services to assure adequate educational opportunities to every child at no direct cost to his family.

Special financial supports should be offered by them to the school districts, singly or in combination, and intermediate units so that no "excess" local cost is involved in providing needed specialized programs of high quality for exceptional children. All state financial charges and aids relating to exceptional children should be of such form that no agency is induced to choose a particular form of education or placement for a child on the basis of financial advantage to itself. Similarly, financial aid patterns should not encourage simple categorizing-labeling of children.

A particular responsibility of state and provincial governments is to provide professional leadership and direction to a carefully planned program of Special Education and to assure cooperation among the several departments of government that may be able to help serve exceptional children and their families.

The Federal Government (United States)[3]

Since an educated and informed citizenry is basic to a democracy, it is the obligation of the Federal Government to make certain that

---

[3]This portion of the document does not necessarily propose any policies for countries other than the United States. Full recognition is extended here to the differences among nations. It is not the intention of this document to attempt to influence any national government other than the United States of America.

every child is provided with a free and equal education. Children are the nation's primary resource and, as such, every child is entitled to an optimal education to maximize his contribution to the continuing development of the nation.

For this reason, there is particular justification for the Federal Government to support aspects of the educational enterprise that cannot reasonably be undertaken and supported individually by the several states. For example, the training of personnel at the most advanced levels and the support of research are activities that probably cannot be well served by the several states or local educational agencies.

Policy:

In general, and in the national interest, the Federal Government should provide major support to programs in the field of Special Education that (1) are a direct Federal responsibility such as programs in Federally operated schools for Indian American children and the education of the dependents in the department of defense programs; or (2) that serve regional or national needs, such as (a) the education of migrant children; (b) the training of leadership personnel to serve as a high-level mobile, national resource; and (c) the maintenance of major research, development, and dissemination activities.

The Federal Government should provide financial supports, including assistance for specialized school construction, to individual and combinations of school districts that wish to provide innovative or exemplary programs for handicapped and gifted children or that, for any reason, enroll an unusually high proportion of children with special needs.

Because the education of exceptional children has, in general, been a neglected area, the Federal Government should provide special categories of support to meet their needs.

The Federal Government should provide a strong source of professional leadership in Special Education with emphasis on the assessment of needs, planning of needed programs, and dissemination of information.

United Nations Resolution

Twenty-sixth session
Agenda item 12

RESOLUTION ADOPTED BY THE GENERAL ASSEMBLY
[on the report of the Third Committee (A/8588)]
2856 (XXVI). *Declaration on the Rights of
Mentally Retarded Persons*

The General Assembly,

Mindful of the pledge of the States Members of the United Nations under the Charter to take joint and separate action in co-operation with the Organization to promote higher standards of living, full employment and conditions of economic and social progress and development,

Reaffirming faith in human rights and fundamental freedoms and in the principles of peace, of the dignity and worth of the human person and of social justice proclaimed in the Charter,

Recalling the principles of the Universal Declaration of Human Rights, the International Covenants on Human Rights,[1] the Declaration of the Rights of the Child[2] and the standards already set for social progress in the constitutions, conventions, recommendations and resolutions of the International Labour Organization, the United Nations Educational, Scientific and Cultural Organization, the

[1] Resolution 2200 A (XXI).
[2] Resolution 1386 (XIV).

103

World Health Organization, the United Nations Children's Fund and of other organizations concerned,

Emphasizing that the Declaration on Social Progress and Development[3] has proclaimed the necessity of protecting the rights and assuring the welfare and rehabilitation of the physically and mentally disadvantaged,

Bearing in mind the necessity of assisting mentally retarded persons to develop their abilities in various fields of activities and of promoting their integration as far as possible in normal life,

Aware that certain countries, at their present stage of development, can devote only limited efforts to this end,

Proclaims this Declaration on the Rights of Mentally Retarded Persons and calls for national and international action to ensure that it will be used as a common basis and frame of reference for the protection of these rights:

1. The mentally retarded person has, to the maximum degree of feasibility, the same rights as other human beings.

2. The mentally retarded person has a right to proper medical care and physical therapy and to such education, training, rehabilitation and guidance as will enable him to develop his ability and maximum potential.

3. The mentally retarded person has a right to economic security and to a decent standard of living. He has a right to perform productive work or to engage in any other meaningful occupation to the fullest possible extent of his capabilities.

4. Whenever possible, the mentally retarded person should live with his own family or with foster parents and participate in different forms of community life. The family with which he lives should receive assistance. If care in an institution becomes necessary, it should be provided in surroundings and other circumstances as close as possible to those of normal life.

5. The mentally retarded person has a right to a qualified guardian when this is required to protect his personal well-being and interests.

6. The mentally retarded person has a right to protection from exploitation, abuse and degrading treatment. If prosecuted for any offense, he shall have a right to due process of law with full recognition being given to his degree of mental responsibility.

7. Whenever mentally retarded persons are unable, because of the severity of their handicap, to exercise all their rights in a meaningful way or it should become necessary to restrict or deny some or all of

---

[3]Resolution 2542 (XXIV).

these rights, the procedure used for that restriction or denial of rights must contain proper legal safeguards against every form of abuse. This procedure must be based on an evaluation of the social capability of the mentally retarded person by qualified experts and must be subject to periodic review and to the right of appeal to higher authorities.

2027th plenary meeting, 20 December 1971.

APPENDIX D

Final Court Order

Pennsylvania Association for Retarded Children, Nancy Beth Bowman et al. v. Commonwealth of Pennsylvania, David H. Kurtzman et al.

In the United States District Court for the Eastern District of Pennsylvania

THE PENNSYLVANIA ASSOCIATION
  FOR RETARDED CHILDREN;
NANCY BETH BOWMAN,
  by her father, Horace Bowman;
LINDA TAUB,
  by her father, Allen Taub;
CHARLES O'LAUGHLIN,
  by his father, Charles O'Laughlin;
CHRISTOPHER JOHN KELLY,
  by his father, JOSEPH KELLY;
MARK MOSER,
  by his father, Clark Moser;
WILLIAM REESE,
  by his father, Edward Reese;
DAVID TUPI,
  by his father, Steven Tupi;
SANDRA LYDARD,
  by her mother, Mrs. Douglas Lydard

CIVIL ACTION
NO. 71–42

EMERY THOMAS,
   by his father, Reginald Thomas;
WILLIAM WENSTON,
   by his father, Robert Wenston;
CINDY MAE HATT,
   by her father, Scott Hatt;
RONALD GREEN,
   by his mother, Mrs. Mattie Green; and
GLENN LOWREY,
   by his father, Richard Lowrey,
on behalf of themselves and all
others similarly situated,

Plaintiffs
v.

COMMONWEALTH OF PENNSYLVANIA;
DAVID H. KURTZMAN, individually and as
   Secretary of Education of the
   Commonwealth of Pennsylvania;
THE STATE BOARD OF EDUCATION of the
   Commonwealth of Pennsylvania;
JOSEPH ADLESTEIN, individually and as
   Acting Secretary of Public Welfare
   of the Commonwealth of Pennsylvania
ABINGTON SCHOOL DISTRICT,
   Montgomery County, Pennsylvania;
PHILADELPHIA SCHOOL DISTRICT,
   Philadelphia, Pennsylvania;
ALLEGHENY COUNTY SCHOOL DISTRICT,
   Allegheny County, Pennsylvania;
WEST HOMESTEAD SCHOOL DISTRICT,
   Allegheny County, Pennsylvania;
BERKS COUNTY SCHOOL DISTRICT,
   Berks County, Pennsylvania;
SHALER TOWNSHIP SCHOOL DISTRICT,
   Allegheny County, Pennsylvania;
GOVERNOR MIFFLIN SCHOOL DISTRICT,
   Berks County, Pennsylvania;
WILSON SCHOOL DISTRICT,
   Berks County, Pennsylvania;
MARPLE-NEWTOWN SCHOOL DISTRICT,
   Delaware County, Pennsylvania;

PITTSBURGH SCHOOL DISTRICT,
  Pittsburgh, Pennsylvania;
READING SCHOOL DISTRICT,
  Berks County, Pennsylvania;
SUSQUEHANNA COUNTY SCHOOL DISTRICT,
  Susquehanna County, Pennsylvania;
MOUNTAIN VIEW SCHOOL DISTRICT,
  Susquehanna County, Pennsylvania;
on behalf of themselves and all other
school districts similarly situated,

Defendants

Opinion, Order, and Injunction

BEFORE ADAMS, CIRCUIT JUDGE; MASTERSON, DISTRICT JUDGE; AND BRODERICK, DISTRICT JUDGE.

MASTERSON, J.

May 5th, 1972

This civil rights case, a class action, was brought by the Pennsylvania Association for Retarded Children[1] and the parents of thirteen individual retarded children on behalf of all mentally retarded persons between the ages 6 and 21 whom the Commonwealth of Pennsylvania, through its local school districts and intermediate units, is presently excluding from a program of education and training in the public schools.[2] Named as defendants are the Commonwealth of Pennsylvania, Secretary of Welfare, State Board of Education and thirteen individual school districts scattered throughout the Commonwealth. In addition, plaintiffs have joined all other school districts in the Commonwealth as class defendants of which the named districts are said to be representative.

The exclusions of retarded children complained of are based upon

---

[1] The Pennsylvania Association for Retarded Children (PARC) and its fifty-three member chapters constitutes an organization which for some 20 years has undertaken part of the burden of educating and training retarded children in the Commonwealth. In addition, PARC has sought to advance the general interests of retarded citizens of Pennsylvania.

[2] The parties have stipulated that when the complaint was filed, all the named plaintiffs were being excluded from any program of public education and training. See, passim, Statement of Uncontested Facts—Docket #97.

four State statutes:[3] (1) 24 *Purd. Stat.* Sec. 13–1375 which relieves the State Board of Education from any obligation to educate a child whom a public school psychologist certifies as uneducable and untrainable. The burden of caring for such a child then shifts to the Department of Welfare which has no obligation to provide any educational services for the child; (2) 24 *Purd. Stat.* Sec. 13–1304 which allows an indefinite postponement of admission to public school of any child who has not attained a mental age of five years; (3) 24 *Purd. Stat.* Sec. 13–1330 which appears to excuse any child from compulsory school attendance whom a psychologist finds unable to profit therefrom; and (4) 24 *Purd. Stat.* Sec. 13–1326 which defines compulsory school age as 8 to 17 years but has been used in practice to postpone admissions of retarded children until age 8 or to eliminate them from public schools at age 17.

Plaintiffs allege that Sections 1375 (uneducable and untrainable) and 1304 (mental age of 5 years) are constitutionally infirm both on their faces and as applied in three broad respects. First, plaintiffs argue that these statutes offend due process because they lack any provision for notice and a hearing before a retarded person is either excluded from a public education or a change is made in his educa-

---

[3]The four state statutes employed by the defendants to exclude retarded children from a public education read as follows:

1. 24 Purd. Stat. Sec. 13–1375.

   "*Uneducable Children Provided for by Department of Public Welfare.* The State Board of Education shall establish standards for temporary or permanent exclusion from the public schools of children who are found to be uneducable and untrainable in the public schools. Any child who is reported by a person who is certificated as a public school psychologist as being uneducable and untrainable in the public schools, may be reported by the board of school directors to the Superintendent of Public Instruction and when approved by him, in accordance with the standards of the State Board of Education shall be certified to the Department of Public Welfare as a child who is uneducable and untrainable in the public schools. When a child is thus certified the public schools shall be relieved of the obligation of providing education or training for such child. The Department of Public Welfare shall thereupon arrange for the care, training, and supervision of such child in a manner not inconsistent with the laws governing mentally defective individuals."

2. 24 Purd. Stat. Sec. 13–1304 provides: "*Admission of Beginners.* . . . The board of school directors may refuse to accept or retain beginners who have not attained a mental age of five years. . . ."

In certain instances this statute results in permanent exclusion since it is theoretically possible for a child with an I.Q. of 35 or below (the I.Q. intelligence test is normally relied upon to establish a mental age) never to achieve a mental age of five years. This result occurs because the I.Q. ratio levels off at chronological age 15. See N.T. 79–80 (August 12 Hearing) (Dr. James Gallagher).

3. 24 Purd. Stat. Sec. 13–1130 provides: "*Exceptions to Compulsory Attendance.* The provisions of this act requiring regular attendance shall not apply to any child who: . . . (2) Has been examined by an approved mental clinic or by a person certificated as a public school psychologist or psychological examiner, and has been found to be unable to profit from further public school attendance, and who has been reported to the board of school directors and excused, in accordance with regulations prescribed by the State Board of Education; . . ."

4. 24 Purd. Stat. Sec. 13–1326 provides: "*Definitions.* The term 'compulsory school age' as hereinafter used, shall mean the period of a child's life from the time the child's parents elect to have the child enter school, which shall be not later than at the age of eight (8) years, until the age of seventeen (17) years."

tional assignment within the public system.[4] Secondly, they assert that the two provisions violate equal protection because the premise of the statutes which necessarily assumes that certain retarded children are uneducable and untrainable lacks a rational basis in fact.[5] Finally, plaintiffs contend that because the Constitution and laws of Pennsylvania guarantee an education to all children,[6] these two sections violate due process in that they arbitrarily and capriciously deny that given right to retarded children. Plaintiffs third contention also raises a pendent question of state law, that is, whether the Pennsylvania Constitution as well as other laws of the Commonwealth already afford them a right to public education.

It is not alleged that Sections 1330 (excusal from compulsory attendance) or 1326 (definition of compulsory school age) are facially defective under the United States Constitution. Rather, plaintiffs contend that these provisions violate due process (lack of a prior hearing) and equal protection (no basis in fact to support exclusion) *as applied* to retarded children.

In addition, plaintiffs contend that the clear intent of Section 1330 is to forgive *parents* from any criminal penalty for what otherwise would be a violation of compulsory attendance requirements, and consequently, use of this provision to *exclude* retarded children constitutes an impermissible misinterpretation of state law. Likewise, plaintiffs assert that Section 1326 relates only to the obligation of *parents* (under penalty of criminal sanctions) to place their chil-

---

[4]In general, the public sector has four possible assignments for the retarded child: regular, retarded-educable, retarded-trainable, and uneducable-untrainable.

[5]Counsel for the plaintiffs asserts in his Memorandum in Support of Plaintiff's Motion to Convene a Three Judge Court that the right to an education, once given, constitutes a fundamental right, and therefore the defendants must show a compelling state interest in order to lawfully exclude retarded children. Cf. *Brown v. Board of Education*, 349 U.S. 294 (1954). Compare, *Shapiro v. Thompson*, 394 U.S. 618, 634 (1969) (travel); *Loving v. Virginia*, 388 U.S. 1, 9 (1967) (race); *Harper v. Virginia State Board of Elections*, 383 U.S. 663, 670 (1966) (voting).

But we are satisfied that the plaintiffs have established a colorable constitutional claim even under the less stringent rational basis test, and consequently we need not decide whether the Commonwealth must demonstrate a compelling state interest in order to dispose of the narrow issues presently before us.

Plaintiffs also allege in their complaint that Sections 1375 and 1304 violate equal protection in that (1) they condition a retarded child's education upon the impermissible criteria of wealth and (2) they require the retarded child's parents to pay additional monies to secure his education even though these parents are taxed for support of a system of public education. Once again, because of our satisfaction with the colorability of equal protection claim apart from possible discrimination against poor persons, we need not face these issues.

[6]Plaintiffs point to Art. 3 §14 of the Pennsylvania Constitution which reads:

"The General Assembly shall provide for the maintenance and support of a thorough and efficient system of public education to serve the needs of the Commonwealth;"
24 Purd. Stat. 13–1301 which provides:

"Every child, being a resident of any school district, between the ages of six (6) and twenty-one (21) years, may attend the public schools in his district, subject to the provision of this Act;"
nd 24 Purd. Stat. 13–1326 which reads in part,

'The term 'compulsory school age,' as hereinafter used, shall mean the period of a child's life from the time the child enters school which shall be not later than at the age of eight (8) years."

dren in public schools, and its use to *exclude* retarded children contravenes the obvious meaning of the statute. To place these questions of state law before us, plaintiffs advance the principle of pendent jurisdiction.

Plaintiffs predicate jurisdiction of this court upon 28 U.S.C. § 1343(3)[7] and their causes of action upon 42 U.S.C. § 1981[8] and § 1983.[9] By way of relief, they seek both a declaratory judgment that the statutes are unconstitutional and a preliminary and permanent injunction against the enforcement of these laws by the defendants.[10] On the basis of these pleadings, it was concluded that the case raised important and substantial federal questions requiring consideration by a three judge court under 28 U.S.C. § 2281.[11]

Shortly after the appointment of the three judge Court by the Chief Judge of the Court of Appeals, we entered an order fixing June 15, 1971 as the hearing date on plaintiffs' motion for a preliminary injunction and June 11, 1971 as the date for prehearing conference. Between the date of our order and June 11th, however, the parties asked for an opportunity to settle amicably at least that part of the case which related to the plaintiffs' demand for due process hearings before exclusion from a public school education or a change in educational assignment within the public system is ordered. To afford them such an opportunity, we vacated our earlier order and postponed the hearing date until August 12th, 1971 and set August 2nd, 1971 as the final pre-hearing conference date.

In the interim, the parties agreed upon a Stipulation which

[7] § 1343. *Civil rights and elective franchise.* The district courts shall have original jurisdiction of any civil action authorized by law to be commenced by any person:

(3) To redress the deprivation, under color of any state law, statute, ordinance, regulation, custom or usage, of any right, privilege or immunity secured by the Constitution of the United States or by any Act of Congress providing for equal rights of citizens or of all persons within the jurisdiction of the United States.

[8] § 1981. *Equal rights under the law.* All persons within the jurisdiction of the United States shall have the same right in every State and Territory to make and enforce contracts, to sue, be parties, give evidence, and to the full and equal benefit of all laws and proceedings for the security of persons and property as is enjoyed by white citizens, and shall be subject to like punishment, pains, penalties, taxes, licenses and exactions of every kind and to no other.

[9] § 1983 *Civil action for deprivation of rights.* Every person, who, under color of any statute, ordinance, regulation, custom, or usage, of any State or Territory, subjects or causes to be subjected, any citizen of the United States or other persons within the jurisdiction thereof to the deprivation of any rights, privileges, or immunities secured by the Constitution and laws, shall be liable to the party injured in an action at law, suit in equity, or other proper proceedings for redress.

[10] See 28 U.S.C.§ § 2201 and 2202.

[11] 28 U.S.C. § 2281. *Injunction against enforcement of State three-judge court required.* An interlocutory or permanent injunction restraining the enforcement, operation or execution of any State statute by restraining the action of any officer of such State in the enforcement or execution of such statute or of an order made by an administrative board or commission acting under state statutes, shall not be granted by any district court or judge thereof upon the ground of the unconstitutionality of such statute unless the application therefore is heard and determined by a district court of three judges under section 2284 of this title.

basically provides that no child who is mentally retarded or thought to be mentally retarded can be assigned initially (or re-assigned) to either a regular or special educational status, or excluded from a public education without a prior recorded hearing before a special hearing officer. At that hearing, parents have the right to representation by counsel, to examine their child's records, to compel the attendance of school officials who may have relevant evidence to offer, to cross-examine witnesses testifying on behalf of school officials and to introduce evidence of their own. On June 18th, this Court entered an interim order approving the Stipulation.

In mid-August, as scheduled, we heard plaintiffs' evidence relating to both the due process and equal protection claims, although the evidence was particularly directed toward the unresolved question of equal protection. Following testimony by four eminent experts in the field of education of retarded children,[12] the parties once again expressed a desire to settle the equal protection dispute by agreement rather than judicial determination. We then suspended further testimony in order to afford the parties time to resolve the remaining issues.

On October 7th, 1971 the parties submitted a Consent Agreement to this Court which, along with the June 18th Stipulation, would settle the entire case. Essentially, this Agreement deals with the four state statutes in an effort to eliminate the alleged equal protection problems. As a proposed cure, the defendants agreed, *inter alia,* that since "the Commonwealth of Pennsylvania has undertaken to provide a free public education for all of its children between the ages of six and twenty-one years" (Paragraph 5), therefore, "it is the Commonwealth's obligation to place each mentally retarded child in a *free, public program of education and training appropriate to the child's capacity*" (Paragraph 7). To effectuate this result without

---

[12]The court heard from (1) *I. Ignacy Goldberg,* who is, *inter alia,* Professor of Education, Department of Special Education, Columbia University; member of the President's Panel on Mental Retardation (1961); consultant to the Children's Bureau, Department of Health, Education and Welfare; Scientific Advisory Board member of the Kennedy Child Study Center, New York; and author or co-author of almost 50 publications on mental retardation; (2) *James J. Gallagher,* who is, *inter alia,* the first Director of the Bureau of Education for the Handicapped and Associate Commissioner of Education, U. S. Office of Education, Department of Health, Education and Welfare (1967–1969); Deputy Assistant Secretary for Program Planning, Research and Education, Department of Health, Education and Welfare; Director, Frank Porter Graham Child Development Center, University of North Carolina; and author or co-author of some 30 publications on the education of retarded persons; (3) *Donald J. Stedman,* who is *inter alia,* first Associate Director of the John F. Kennedy Center for Research on Education and Human Development, Peabody College; Professor and Chairman of the Division of Human Development in the School of Education, University of North Carolina; Associate Editor of the Journal of Mental Deficiency; author or co-author of some 30 publications on the mentally retarded; and a permanent consultant to the President's Committee on Mental Retardation; and (4) *Burton Blatt,* who is *inter alia,* Centennial Professor and Director, Division of Special Education and Rehabilitation, Syracuse University; member of the first Connecticut State Advisory Counsel on Mental Retardation; member of the State of New York Committee for Children; member of the National Advisory Committee of the R & D Center for Handicapped Children of Teachers College, Columbia University; and author or co-author of almost 90 publications.

conceding the unconstitutionality of the foregoing statutes or upsetting the existing statutory scheme, the Attorney General of the Commonwealth agreed to issue Opinions declaring in substance that: (1) Section 1375 means that "insofar as the Department of Public Welfare is charged to arrange for the care, training and supervision of a child certified to it, the Department of Public Welfare must provide a program of education and training appropriate to the capacities of that child" (Paragraph 37); (2) Section 1304 means "*only* that a school district may refuse to accept into or retain in the lowest grade of the *regular* primary school [as contrasted with a *special* primary school] any child who has not attained a mental age of five years" (Paragraph 10); (3) Section 1330(2) means "*only* that a parent may be excused from liability under the compulsory attendance provisions of the School Code when, with the approval of the local school board and the Secretary of Education and the finding by an approved school psychologist, the parent elects to withdraw the child from attendance; Section 1330(2) may not be used by defendants, contrary to parents' wishes, to terminate or in any way deny access to a free public program of education and training to any mentally retarded child" (Paragraph 20); and (4) Section 1326 means "*only* that parents of a child have a compulsory duty while the child is between eight and seventeen years of age to assure his attendance in a program of education and training; and Section 1326 does not limit the ages between which a child must be granted access to a free public program of education and training [and may not be used as such]" (Paragraph 16). Thus, possible use of these four provisions to exclude (or postpone) retarded children from a program of public education was effectively foreclosed by this Agreement. And on October 22, 1971, the Attorney General issued these agreed upon Opinions.

In addition, the Consent Agreement addresses itself to three other matters involving the education of retarded children which the plaintiffs did not specifically raise in their pleadings. First, in the area of pre-school education, the defendants agreed to cease applying 24 *Purd. Stat.* Sec. 13–1371[13] so as to deny retarded children below the age of six access to a free pre-school program of education and training appropriate to their learning capacities whenever the school districts provide such a preschool program to *normal* children below the age of six. The Attorney General again issued an Opinion so interpreting Section 1371(1).

Next, the defendants agreed to cease applying 24 *Purd. Stat.* Sec.

---

[13]24 Purd. Stat. Sec. 13–1371(1):

"*Definition of exceptional children; reports; examination.*

(1) The term 'exceptional children' shall mean children of school age who deviate from the average in physical, mental, emotional or social characteristics to such an extent that they require special educational facilities or services and shall include all children in detention homes."

13–1376[14] so as to deny tuition or tuition maintenance to any mentally retarded person. Basically, Section 1376 provides for the payment of tuition to private schools by the Commonwealth and local school districts (75% and 25% respectively) where, with the approval of the Department of Education, a child afflicted with blindness, deafness, cerebral palsy, brain damage or muscular dystrophy is attending a private school. Prior to the Consent Agreement, this statute was interpreted not to apply to retarded children unless they also suffered from one of the maladies mentioned above. Consequently, if the public sector excluded a retarded child (who lacked a multiple disability) under Section 1375, 1304, 1330 or 1326, his parents had to assume the full financial burden of educating and training him in a private school. Often, because of the special care required, this burden assumed formidable proportions.[15] Thus, the Attorney General issued an Opinion "construing the term 'brain

[14]24 Purd. Stat. Sec. 13–1376:
"Cost of tuition and maintenance of certain exceptional children in approved institutions.

(a) When a child between the ages of six (6) and twenty-one (21) years of age resident in this Commonwealth, who is blind or deaf, or afflicted with cerebral palsy and/or brain damage and/or muscular dystrophy, is enrolled, with the approval of the Department of Public Instruction, as a pupil in any of the schools or institutions for the blind or deaf, or cerebral palsied and/or brain damaged and/or muscular dystrophied, under the supervision of, subject to the review of or approved by the Department of Public Instruction, in accordance with standards and regulations promulgated by the Council of Basic Education, the School District in which such child is resident shall pay twenty-five per centum (25%) of the cost of tuition and maintenance of such child in such school or institution, as determined by the Department of Public Instruction; and the Commonwealth shall pay, out of funds appropriated to the department for special education, seventy-five per centum (75%) of the cost of their tuition and maintenance, as determined by the Department."

[15]Leonard Kalish, Esq., appearing *pro se* on behalf of his fifteen year old daughter who is a member of the plaintiff class stated that his child has been excluded from a public education all of her life. He continued:

"I would just like to call to the Court's attention what the realities of that situation are, and I think I can speak with some authority because for the last nine years, my fifteen year old daughter has been denied access to public education without due process, but consistently denied, and as a result of which we have had her in private schools for the last nine years.

"Now in those nine years, not counting the present year, not counting the year which started last summer, we have spent approximately forty thousand dollars on her private schooling, shall I say. At the present time we have her in a private school, a residential school where we pay a tuition of twelve thousand dollars a year, not counting the extras of which there are considerable extras, and I want to say to the Court that what I am saying here to to our situation is paralled by many other situations of many other children, and their parents.

"Now if a public facility were established that comes anywhere near striking the distance of appropriateness for my child, Your Honors can rest assured that I will welcome that public facility with open arms. The financial burden of giving my child private education is very considerable. There is no pride or status symbol involved in having a child in a private school such as the private schools to which my child and others in the same situation would go. In other words, it isn't out of any feeling of status that I am undertaking this heavy financial burden. It is simply because there is no public facility.

"Now the moment a public facility is indicated, even just on the drawing board or on brochures, or papers of any kind which will look reasonably appropriate, I will assure Your Honors that ninety-five per cent or more of all parents will rush to get their children in there because everyone of the parents is laboring under a backbreaking financial burden. We're not talking about wealthy people here. We are talking about ordinary people, and I know a great many of them who send their children to the same school where I send mine, and I have had my child in one other school before this, and I have had her with a private tutor for a year."

damage' as used in Section 1376 . . . so as to include thereunder all mentally retarded persons, thereby making available to them tuition for day school and tuition and maintenance for residential school . . . " (Paragraph 27).

Finally, the defendants agreed to cease applying 24 *Purd. Stat.* Sec. 13–1372(3)[16] so as "to deny [mentally retarded children] homebound instruction under that Section . . . merely because no physical disability accompanies the retardation or because retardation is not a short-term disability" (Paragraph 31). Once again, the Attorney General issued an Opinion so construing this provision.

The lengthy Consent Agreement concludes by stating that "[e]very retarded person between the ages of six and twenty-one shall be provided access to a free public program of education and training appropriate to his capacities as soon as possible but in no event later than *September 1, 1972*" (Paragraph 42). To implement the agreed upon relief and assure that it would be extended to all members of this class, Dennis E. Haggerty, Esq., a distinguished member of the Pennsylvania Bar who has devoted much of his energy to the welfare of retarded children, and Dr. Herbert Goldstein, an eminent expert in the education of retarded children who is Professor and Director of the Curriculum Research and Development Center in Mental Retardation at the Ferkauf Graduate School of Humanities and Social Sciences, Yeshiva University, were appointed Masters at the expense of the Commonwealth (Paragraph 45). Next, the Consent Agreement charges defendants with the duty within 30 days, to formulate and submit to the Masters a plan to locate, evaluate and give notice to all members of the plaintiff class (Paragraph 47). Finally, and perhaps most importantly, the Agreement states that:

The defendants shall formulate and submit to the Masters for their approval *a plan to be effectuated by September 1, 1972,* to commence or recommence a free public program of education and training for all mentally retarded persons . . . aged between four and twenty-one years as of the date of this Order, and for all mentally retarded persons of such ages hereafter. The plan shall specify the range of programs of education and training, there [sic] kind and number, necessary to provide an appropriate program of education and training to all mentally retarded children, where they shall be conducted, arrangements for their financing, and, if additional teachers are found to

[16]24 Purd. Stat. Section 1372(3)
"Standards; plans; special classes or schools.
. . . (3) Special Classes or Schools Established and Maintained by School Districts.
". . . If . . . it is not feasible to form a special class in any district or to provide such education for any [exceptional] child in the public schools of the district, the board of school directors of the district shall secure such proper education and training outside the public schools of the district or in special institutions, or by providing for teaching the child in his home. . . . "

be necessary, the plan shall specify recruitment, hiring, and training arrangements (Paragraph 49) (emphasis added).

Thus, if all goes according to plan, Pennsylvania should be providing a meaningful program of education and training to every retarded child in the Commonwealth by September, 1972.

We then entered an *interim order,* without prejudice, pending notice to the class of plaintiffs and the class of defendants, which temporarily enjoined the defendants from applying (1) 24 Purd Stat. Sections 13-1375, 1304, 1330(2), and 1371(1) "so as to deny any mentally retarded child access to a free public program of education and training;" (2) Section 13–1376 "so as to deny tuition or tuition and maintenance to any mentally retarded person except on the same terms as may be applied to other exceptional children, including brain damaged children generally;" and (3) Section 13–1372(3) "[so as to deny] homebound instruction to any mentally retarded person merely because no physical disability accompanies the retardation or because it is not a short-term disability."[17]

Next, in accordance with Rule 23(e), *F.R. Civ. P.,*[18] a hearing was scheduled on any objections to the proposed settlement Agreements. We instructed the named plaintiffs and defendants to notify all remaining members of their respective classes (primarily by newspaper in the case of plaintiffs and by direct mailing for the defendants). Proper notice went out to the plaintiffs and only one appeared at the hearing.[19] None of the remaining defendants appeared, however, because the Commonwealth neglected to send them any notice.[20] Consequently, we ordered that new notice be given, and rescheduled the hearing for November 12, 1971.

Notice of that hearing went out about October 29th,[21] and Philip Salkin, Esq. and William B. Arnold, Esq. appeared and filed

---

[17]Our power to enter an injunction does not stem from a finding that the State statutes contravene the United States Constitution or that the state officers acted in an unconstitutional manner. We make no such findings in this opinion. We hold, however, that the plaintiffs have established a colorable constitutional claim (see pages 123–128, infra), and hence the court has jurisdiction under 28 U.S.C. § 1343(3). Once jurisdiction is established, we then have the judicial power necessary to approve and enforce a settlement agreement. See *Kelly v. Greer,* 365 F. 2d 669 (3rd Cir. 1966), *cert. denied,* 385 U.S. 1035 (1967); *Berger v. Grace Line, Inc.,* _____ F. Supp. _____ (E. D. Pa. 1972). On this basis, we issued the Injunction to insure that all school districts and intermediate units in the Commonwealth would clearly understand that this class action binds them to follow our Order approving the settlement.

[18]23(e) *Dismissal or Compromise.* A class action shall not be dismissed or compromised without the approval of the court, and notice of the proposed dismissal or compromise shall be given to all members of the class in such manner as the court directs.

[19]Mr. Leonard Kalish, Esq. appeared on behalf of his daughter, a member of the plaintiff class. He did not object to the substance of the proposed Consent Agreement, but only questioned the absence of a precise definition of mental retardation. His motion was later compromised, and he has withdrawn his objection.

[20]N. T. at 4–7 (Hearing of October 22, 1971).

[21]N.T. at 40 (Hearing of November 12, 1971).

objections on behalf of the Montgomery County Intermediate Unit and the Lancaster-Lebanon Intermediate Unit respectively. In addition, John D. Killian, Esq. appeared and objected for the Pennsylvania Association of Private Schools for Exceptional Children.

Both attorneys for the Intermediate Units argued to the Court that the notice they received was inadequate to prepare their cases against both the Stipulation of June 18th and the Consent Agreement of October 7th.[22] They also argued that many districts and intermediate units failed to appear because they did not have enough time to analyze and react to the two rather lengthy and intricate proposals. The attorneys pointed out that since most school boards meet on the first week of each month, these bodies would not even have an opportunity to review the documents until after December 1st.[23]

To extend every element of fairness in this important litigation, we ordered that a *second individual notice* be sent to all 29 intermediate units and 569 school districts, extending them an opportunity to object and be heard at yet another hearing on December 15, 1971. Following this second notice, the Allegheny Intermediate Unit No. 3, Chester County Intermediate Unit No. 24, Schuylkill Intermediate Unit No. 29, Delaware County Intermediate Unit, and 9 individual school districts within these four Units joined the opponents of the settlement.

On December 15th and 16th, we heard from the objectors and their witnesses. Essentially, the complaining defendants challenged parts of the June 18th Stipulation (dealing with due process hearings) which they claimed were unnecessary, burdensome and administratively unwieldy and impractical.[24] The wisdom of a few minor portions of the October 7th Consent Agreement was also questioned.[25] Apart from questioning certain details of the Agreements, the objectors challenged our jurisdiction over the case and over themselves as purported members of a class. Finally, they raised the issue of abstention.

Following this testimony, the proponents of the settlement met with the objectors in an effort to modify the two documents so as to satisfy every one involved. Intensive negotiations ensued. Final legal argument was scheduled for January 31, 1972.

---

[22]*Id.* at 45.

[23]*Id.* at 48.

[24]For example, the original Stipulation provided for *two* notices to the parents of their right to a hearing and made no provision for waiver of the hearing. The objecting defendants took issue with these features.

[25]For example, the defendants disagreed with the need for an automatic reevaluation of retarded children in special classes every two years and the mandatory requirement that homebound instruction involve education and training for at least five hours a week.

At the request of the litigants, we postponed final argument until February 7, 1972. On that date, only *one* defendant remained—the Lancaster-Lebanon Intermediate Unit. All others had withdrawn their objections because subsequent modifications of the Stipulation and Consent Agreement by the proponents satisfied their complaints.[26] The Pennsylvania Association of Private Schools for Exceptional Children (which is not a member of either class) also expressed dissatisfaction at that hearing.

The arguments presented by Lancaster-Lebanon are essentially legal, that is, the Intermediate Unit does not question the *fairness* of the proposed settlement to the members of either class,[27] rather it seeks to destroy the Agreements altogether by raising the issue of jurisdiction as well as the oft-mentioned, but seldom fully understood, issue of abstention.

I. Jurisdiction

A. *Controversy Under Article III*

Preliminarily, the issue of whether the Lancaster-Lebanon Intermediate Unit can even raise jurisdictional issues at a hearing on the proposed settlement of a class action under Rule 23(e) arises. Theoretically, the scope of such a hearing is limited to an inquiry into the fairness of the settlement. See *Moore's Federal Practice*, § 23.80(4). Since jurisdictional issues relate to the very power of this court to hear this case and bind the parties, however, we think that the objectors must be permitted to raise them.

Although not particularly pressed at final oral argument (which was devoted primarily to abstention), Lancaster-Lebanon has raised two distinct jurisdictional issues throughout this litigation. First, Lancaster-Lebanon charges that there is no controversy before this court within the meaning of Article III, Sec. 2 of the United States Constitution because of alleged collusion and total agreement on the merits between the plaintiffs and the Commonwealth in conducting

---

[26]An Amended Stipulation and Amended Consent Agreement were filed with this Court on February 18, 1972. The general import of these documents, however, remained the same as explained in our extended analysis above; therefore, we need not review them again.

[27]"[T]his Intermediate Unit approves the *general aims* of the interim order to improve the education and training opportunities of mentally retarded children. . . ." *Objections by Lancaster-Lebanon Intermediate Unit No. 13* at 1 (emphasis original); "[W]e agree with the general aims, of course we do. It is an enlightened objective."

(N.T. 26 49—Hearing of November 12, 1971) (Statement of William B. Arnold, Esq.). In response to Judge Masterson's questioning, Mr. Arnold did not cite any specific objections to any provisions of the Consent Agreement. (N.T. at 43—Hearing of February 7, 1972.)

this suit. Secondly, the Intermediate Unit contends that this Court lacks jurisdiction to bind it to any Consent Agreement because the Lancaster-Lebanon Unit received no notice and had no opportunity to appear when the suit was first instituted. (See Section I.B, infra.). We find both contentions without merit.

Undoubtedly, if two litigants commence a suit with the same goals in mind, no controversy exists to give the district court jurisdiction as required by Article III, Sec. 2. See *Moore v. Charlotte-Mecklenburg Board of Education*, 402 U.S. 47 (1971); *United States v. Johnson*, 319 U.S. 302 (1943); *Muskrat v. United States*, 219 U.S. 346 (1911). But a different case arises when litigants *begin* a suit as adversaries, and then at some later point decide to compromise the dispute. In such an instance, the court does not *ipso facto* lose jurisdiction over the matter for want of a controversy. Cf. *Dixon v. Attorney General of Com. of Pa.*, 325 F. Supp. 966 (E.D. Pa. 1971) (Biggs, Circuit Judge). This latter rule flows from common sense as well as the fact that even in preparing a compromise, the parties may remain adversaries within the meaning of Article III.

The record in this case clearly shows that the Commonwealth did not collaborate with the plaintiffs in bringing or conducting this suit. Indeed, from January until June, 1971, the Attorney General and the thirteen named school districts vigorously contested every phase of plaintiffs' case. First, the Commonwealth filed motions to dismiss which were accompanied by elaborate briefs. The defendants denied jurisdiction, denied that a claim had been stated upon which relief might be granted, denied that plaintiffs had raised a substantial federal question, and questioned whether PARC had standing to sue. On the merits, they asserted that all of the statutes attacked were founded upon rational bases.[28] Subsequently, the defendants filed a 13 page brief opposing plaintiffs' motion to convene a three-judge court. Moreover, in discovery, the defendants resisted the production of certain documents and the parties had to appeal to this Court for resolution of the dispute.

In June, 1971, it is true, the parties agreed to settle the issue of due process hearings. Even so, the defendants did not give the plaintiffs carte blanche to draw up any proposal of their choosing; rather the

---

[28]"The reasonableness of this distinction is so clear as to admit of no argument. A child who is uneducable and untrainable requires treatment different from those children of the other classifications. To place the retarded child in the public classroom is to subject such child to frustration since he cannot compete mentally with the other children, to subject him to ridicule by other students, to generally disrupt the classroom, albeit not intentionally and to impose upon the teacher a burden with which he is not trained to cope. There is therefore sound reason for the distinction made by Section 1375 of the School Code."—*Commonwealth's Brief in Support of Motion to Dismiss* at 3 (Docket #22.).

arts of negotiation and compromise were employed, with Commonwealth experts in the field of education also taking part in the discussions.[29]

Despite negotiations on this front, the defendants steadfastly adhered to their original position on plaintiffs' equal protection claims. Indeed, it was not until after a day of testimony from four distinguished experts that the Commonwealth agreed to relent on this issue as well. Far from an indication of collusion, however, the Commonwealth's willingness to settle this dispute reflects an intelligent response to overwhelming evidence against their position.

Once the compromise was prepared, of course, plaintiffs and the named defendants shared identical interests in seeking approval of the settlement. Nevertheless, because these defendants refused to concede the unconstitutionality of the statutes and continued to enforce them, the parties remained adversaries on the constitutional issues which are critical to our jurisdiction. Hence, we conclude that a controversy exists under Article III, Sec. 2.

B. Over the Parties

Next, Lancaster-Lebanon argues that it is not bound by these Consent Agreements or the Injunction because this Court lacks jurisdiction, not necessarily over the subject matter, but over it as a party. The Intermediate Unit predicates this assertion upon the concept that under the Due Process Clause, notice at the commencement of the litigation constitutes a prerequisite to a court's jurisdiction over the parties. As applied to the facts of this case, however, we disagree.

We begin by holding that the *defendants* constitute a class under Rule 23(b) (1) (B), *F.R. Civ. P.* This section is appropriate because, as a practical matter, once the issues are decided against one school district within an intermediate unit, or one intermediate unit within the Commonwealth all other districts or intermediate units will ultimately be bound by the result. In other words, "adjudications with respect to individual members of the class, [would] as a practical matter be dispositive of the interests of the other members not parties to the adjudication . . . " Rule 23(b) (1) (B). This result follows because (1) intermediate units have an obligation to coordinate the education of exceptional children where member school districts are unable to sustain individual programs, and (2) the Commonwealth, for reasons of economy and administration, must necessarily maintain a uniform set of rules and regulations govern-

[29]N.T. at 164–176 (Hearing of December 15, 1971) (William Ortman, cross examination).

ing the responsibilities of *all* school districts and intermediate units within the state.[30]

The notice of requirements for a (b)(1) class are set forth in Rule 23(d)(2) which provides as follows:

(d) Orders in Conduct of action. In the conduct of actions to which this rule applies, the court may make appropriate orders. . . . (2) requiring, for the protection of members of the class or otherwise for the fair conduct of the action, that notice be given in such manner as the court may direct to some or all of the members of any step in the action, or of the proposed extent of the judgment. . . .

Under this rule, notice of the litigation to members of the class is apparently discretionary, and "[i]n the degree that there is cohesiveness or unity in the class and the representation is effective, the need for notice to the class will tend toward a minimum."[31] Indeed, most courts have held that where a class is adequately represented, no notice of the suit need be given under the Due Process Clause in order to bind all members of the class. See *Management T.V. Sys. Inc. v. National Football League*, 52 F.R.D. 162 (E.D. Pa. 1971); *Northern Natural Gas Co. v. Grounds*, supra.[32]

But we need not go this far, because the due process issue presented here is significantly different. In this case, the Lancaster-Lebanon Unit, and all 29 other intermediate units and 569 school districts received *two* notices of this proceeding and *two* opportunities to appear before this Court (November 12th and December 15th) *prior* to any final judgment on the fairness of the settlement proposals. And at these hearings, the defendants had an opportunity to recall any expert witness who testified at the August 12th hearing (at which the objectors were not present) for purposes of cross examination. Yet the defendants declined this invitation. In addition, we allowed them an opportunity to present contrary evidence on the merits, and the objecting defendants did produce the testimony which they felt was relevant. All then rested on the record.[33] Since the defendants had an adequate notice to appear and a meaningful opportunity to present evidence *before* we rendered final judgment

[30]The defendant class may also properly fall 23(b) (2) which requires that:
"the party opposing the class [of defendants] [i.e. the plaintiff class] has acted or refused to act on grounds generally applicable to the class [of defendants] [e.g. the plaintiffs have acted in such a way that the defendants are excluding them from public schools] making appropriate final injunctive relief or corresponding declaratory relief with respect to the class of [defendants] as a whole."

[31]Advisory Committee's Note of 1966. See generally, *Moore's Federal Practice* § 23.72.

[32]But see *Eisen v. Carlisle & Jacquelin*, 391 F.2d 555 (2nd Cir. 1968), criticized *Moore's Federal Practice*, § 23.72

[33]N.T. at 78 (Hearing of November 12, 1971); N.T. at 368 (Hearing of December 16, 1971).

on the settlement, we hold that the objecting defendants were afforded every element of procedural due process. See *Armstrong v. Manzo*, 380 U.S. 545,552 (1965).

Further, we are satisfied that the Attorney General adequately represented the interests of all the defendants before the objectors entered the case. To the extent that inadequate representation during the early stages of litigation might constitute a denial of due process,[34] no such denial occurred in this case. By express agreement of counsel, the Attorney General assumed the arduous task of defending this action on behalf of the thirteen named school districts as well as the named officials. And the interests of these named school districts fairly reflected the interests of all school districts in the Commonwealth. Hence, the requirement that the class representatives not have interests antagonistic to those of other members of the class whom they are representing was satisfied.

We have already reviewed the actions of the Attorney General in defending this case. And while conducting their defense, the Commonwealth kept the named parties fully informed of the progress of the litigation and advised them of the content of the proposed settlements.[35] Considering these facts, we reject Lancaster-Lebanon's attacks upon our jurisdiction over the parties.

C. Over the Subject Matter

Although no party questions the quality of plaintiffs' constitutional claims, it is basic constitutional law that federal district courts cannot acquire jurisdiction over the subject matter of a dispute by consent. Rather our jurisdiction (power) necessarily depends upon the United States Constitution and Acts of Congress. For this reason, consensus of the parties cannot interfere with our fundamental obligation to act only where the Constitution and Congress permit. Cf. *Sibron v. New York*, 392 U.S. 40, 58 (1968); *Young v. United States*, 315 U.S. 257, 258–59 (1942). Consequently, we conclude that this court has a constitutional obligation to examine the record independently and satisfy ourselves that plaintiffs' claims are not "wholly insubstantial and frivolous." *Bell v. Hood*, 327 U.S. 678, 682–83 (1946).

Such an inquiry becomes particularly important in the case of these defendants because we have entered an injunction which, by its terms, binds *all* school districts and intermediate units in the Commonwealth. Moreover, this injunction affects the enforcement

[34]See *Moore's Federal Practice* §23.55.

[35]See Statement of Representation by the Attorney General—Docket No. 98.

of some half-dozen statutes by state officers. The injunctive power of this court must not be used lightly, especially when it operates against state statutes and officers.

We begin with the contention that due process requires a hearing before retarded children may be denied a public education. It is not disputed that prior to this suit, parents of retarded children who are plaintiffs were not afforded a hearing or, in many instances, even notice of their child's exclusion from public school.[36] For example, the parents of David Tupi, a retarded child, were never officially informed of the decision to exclude him from school. Rather, they were only made aware of the situation when the school bus which regularly brought him to school failed to show up.[37] Such crass and summary treatment of these children becomes suspect, we think, because of the stigma which our society unfortunately attaches to the label of mental retardation.[38] Dr. Goldberg testified at length concerning the historical roots of the stigma.[39]

Organized efforts to educate the mentally retarded began about 1848 with the establishment of residential centers which were geared toward preparing mentally retarded individuals for a greater contribution to society as well as sheltering these individuals from a hostile society. About 1900, special education classes for the mentally retarded were started in public schools. These classes were originally denominated "opportunity classes," which indicated that the child was merely waiting somewhere to join the mainstream of the school life.

But Dr. Goldberg stated that in the next decade:

[T]he wonderful idea of adjusting the individuals to our society became the dumping grounds for children who could not manage in other classes and started to be called classes for the feeble-minded, classes for idiots, and so on. . . .

And then the Eugenic Association in the United States started to raise quite a lot of cry that the American Society is going to pieces, mental retardation is hereditary, mentally retardeds are criminals, are prostitutes as the [I.Q.] tests proved. Therefore, something very drastic has to be done.

---

[36]*Statement of Uncontested Facts*, Paragraph #145 at 27. *All* of the defendants are bound by this statement. At the December 15th hearing, we afforded the objectors two weeks to challenge any part of the uncontested facts (which were prepared by the Attorney General and the plaintiffs). Yet no objector requested a hearing at the expiration of the two weeks period.

[37]Statement of Uncontested Facts, Paragraph 90, at 18.

[38]See generally M. Garrison, Jr. and D. Hammill, "Who Are the Retarded," *Exceptional Children*, October 9, 1971; J. Mercer, *The Use and Misuse of Labelling Human Beings: The Ethics of Testing*, unpublished essay presented at an International Symposium on Human Rights, Retardation and Research, Washington, D.C. (1971); President's Committee, *Mental Retardation 1969 Annual Report*; N.T. at 8 (Hearing of August 12, 1971) (Ignacy Goldberg).

[39]N.T. at 10–15 (Hearing of August 12, 1971). The historical summary which follows is a paraphrased summary of his testimony.

And in 1912, the Eugenic Society, the Research Section of the Eugenic Society, namely, the American Breeders Association, suggested that drastic measures be taken to prevent the Americans from becoming all feebleminded [such as] segregation or segregation during the reproductive period, for women, . . . organizing institutions for feeble-minded women of childbearing age in order to prevent them from having children, . . . compulsory sterilization law for women, and castration for men. . . . Another recommendation was euthanasia. This, of course, just introduced and I hope was not implemented.[40] . . . I really want to point out that the days we are talking about are not so far removed, that the stigma attached to mental retardation is still with us, with the general public.[41]

Empirical studies show that stigmatization is a major concern among parents of retarded children. Some parents liken it to a "sentence of death."[42]

Experts agree that it is primarily the *school* which imposes the mentally-retarded label and concomitant stigmatization upon children, either initially or later on through a change in educational assignment. This follows from the fact that the school constitutes the first social institution with which the child comes into contact.[43]

Not only is the school the institution which normally imposes the stigma; sometimes, and perhaps quite often, a child is incorrectly labeled. A recent study of 378 educable mentally retarded students from 36 independent school districts in the five county Greater Philadelphia Area found that "the diagnosis for 25% of the youngsters found in classes for the [educable mentally] retarded may be

---

[40]In *Buck v. Bell*, 274 U.S. 200, 207 (1926), Justice Oliver Wendell Holmes upheld the validity of Virginia's compulsory sterilization law with these words:

> "We have seen more than once that the public welfare may call upon the best citizens for their lives. It would be strange if it could not call upon those who already sap the strength of the State for these lesser sacrifices, often not felt to be such by those concerned, in order to prevent our being swamped with incompetence. It is better for all the world, if instead of waiting to execute degenerate offspring for a crime, or to let them starve for their imbecility, society can prevent those who are manifestly unfit from continuing their kind. . . . Three generations of imbeciles are enough."

The Pennsylvania legislature passed the first such sterilization law in the United States in 1905, but the Governor vetoed it. See Challener, The Law of Sexual Sterilization in Pennsylvania, 57 *Dick. L. Rev.* 298 (1952). During the next decade after *Buck v. Bell*, twenty states passed sterilization statutes. See Note, Human Sterilization, 35 *Iowa L. Rev.* 251, 253 n.12 (1950). During the last thirty years, thirty-two states have had sterilization statutes but five have been declared unconstitutional. O'Hare and Sanks, Eugenic Sterilization, 45 *Geo. L.J.* 30 (1956). See generally, F. Lindman and D. McIntyre, *The Mentally Disabled and the Law* (1961)

[41]N.T. at 11–12 (Hearing of August 12, 1971). Dr. Goldberg went on to outline the progress in education of retarded children since the 1920's. He particularly emphasized the progress made during the 1960's, but reminded us that the stigma remains.

[42]J. Mercer, *The Use and Misuse of Labelling Human Beings: The Ethics of Testing*, supra note 38 at 6.

[43]*Id.* at 2; J. Cohen, Vocational Rehabilitation of the Mentally Retarded, *Pediatric Clinics of North America*, Vol. 15, No. 4 (November 1968) at 1017; N.T., *passim* (Hearing of August 12, 1971).

considered erroneous. An additional 43% may be questioned."[44] The authors conclude: "[O]ne cannot help but be concerned about the consequences of subjecting these children to the 'retarded' curriculum. . . . The stigma of bearing the label 'retarded' is bad enough, but to bear the label when placement is questionable or outright erroneous is an intolerable situation."[45]

In the recent case of *Wisconsin v. Constantineau*, 400 U.S. 433 (1971), the United States Supreme Court considered the necessity of a due process hearing before the state stigmatizes any citizen. There the police, without notice to her or a prior hearing, had posted a notice in all retail liquor establishments forbidding sales to Mrs. Constantineau because of her "excessive drinking." The Court wrote:

> The only issue present here is whether the label or characterization given a person by "posting," though a mark of illness to some, is to others such a stigma or badge of disgrace that procedural due process requires notice and an opportunity to be heard. We agree with the district court that the private interest is such that those requirements . . . must be met. *Id.* at 436.

Considering just *Constantineau* and the evidence presented here, we are convinced that the plaintiffs have established a colorable claim under the Due Process Clause.[46]

Our jurisdiction over plaintiffs' equal protection claims also stands on firm ground. Without exception, expert opinion indicates that:

> [A]ll mentally retarded persons are capable of benefitting from a program of education and training;[47] that the greatest number of retarded persons, given such education and training, are capable of achieving self-sufficiency and the remaining few, with such education and training are capable of

---

[44]M. Garrison, Jr. and D. Hammill, Who are the Retarded, *supra* note 38 at 18.

[45]*Id.* at 20. Dr. Lester Mann who is Special Educator and School Psychologist in Montgomery County estimated that a "significant error" in terms of measurement psychological tests would occur an average in 5% of the cases. (See N.T. at 296—Hearing of December 16, 1971.) The higher figures in the Philadelphia study may be due to the fact that it was conducted in an urban center as well as the fact that Garrison and Hamill employed five different measures in their tests.

[46]For this reason we need not consider the colorability of plaintiffs' claim that education constitutes an essential interest, and therefore it may not be disturbed by government action without a prior hearing. See, e.g., *Wasson v. Towbridge*, 382 F.2d 807 (2nd Cir. 1967); *Woods v. Wright*, 334 F.2d 369 (5th Cir. 1964); *Dixon v. Alabama State Board of Education*, 294 F.2d 150 (5th Cir. 1961); *Stricklin v. Regents of Univ. of Wisconsin*, 297 F. Supp. 416 (W.D. Wis. 1969). See also, *Goldberg v. Kelly*, 397 U.S. 254 (1970) (public assistance benefits); *Snaidach v. Family Finance Corp.*, 395 U.S. 337 (1969) (prejudgment garnishment); *Schware v. Board of Bar Examiners*, 353 U.S. 232 (1957) (right to take bar examination); *Slochower v. Board of Higher Education*, 350 U.S. 551 (1956) (dismissal from employment); *Goldsmith v. United States Board of Tax Appeals*, 270 U.S. 117 (1926) (accountant's qualifications to practice before the Board of Tax Appeals).

[47]N. T. at 18 (Goldberg), 63 (Gallagher), 115 (Stedman), 137 (Blatt) (Hearing of August 12, 1971); N. T. at 248 (Mann) (Hearing of December 16, 1971).

achieving some degree of self-care;[48] that the earlier such education and training begins, the more thoroughly and the more efficiently a mentally retarded person will benefit from it[49] and, whether begun early or not, that a mentally retarded person can benefit at any point in his life and development from a program of education.[50] *Consent Agreement*, Paragraph 4.

Despite this evidence and despite the fact that Pennsylvania provides an education to most children, the State's *1965 Pennsylvania Mental Retardation Plan* estimates that while 46,000 school age retarded children were enrolled in public schools, another 70,000 to 80,000 retarded children between the ages of 5 and 21 were denied access to *any* public education services in schools, home or day care or other community facilities, or state residential institutions (C.M.R.P. at 4, 92, 93, 142).[51]

Because of an absence of adequate resources, facilities and teachers as well as the lack of a structured plan, even those whom the State serves in its institutions (i.e., residential centers, hospitals, etc.) do not always benefit. For example, Dr. Edward R. Goldman, Commissioner of the Office of Mental Retardation, Department of Welfare, testified that there are presently 4,159 children of school age in state institutions. But only 100 of these children are in a full program of education and training; 1,700 are in partial but inadequate programs, and 3,259 are in no program of any kind.[52] Moreover, the *1965 Pennsylvania Mental Retardation Plan* reports that because of a lack of space, the State housed 900 mentally

---

[48]N.T. at 668–68 (Gallagher).

The President's Committee on Mental Retardation in its *1969 Annual Report* at 17 estimates that "[S]ome three-quarters of this nation's retarded people could become self-supporting if given the right kind of training early enough. Another 10 to 15 percent could become partially self-supporting."

Dr. Aubrey J. Yates in *Behavior Therapy* (1970) at 234 states that "[T]wo-thirds and probably four-fifths of those who might on I.Q. be classified as feeble minded can live in financial and social independence under present economic circumstances." See generally, President's Committee on Mental Retardation, *These Too, Must be Equal;* J. Cohen, *Vocational Rehabilitation of the Mentally Retarded, supra* note 43.

[49]N.T. at 30 (Goldberg), 73 (Gallagher) (Hearing of August 12, 1971). See generally, CEC Policy Statement, *Journal of Exceptional Children* 423–24 (February 1971); President's Committee on Mental Retardation, *1969 Annual Report; 1965 Pennsylvania Mental Retardation Plan;* President's Committee on Mental Retardation, *The Six Hour Retarded Child* (1970).

[50]N.T. at 30 (Goldberg) (Hearing of August 12, 1971).

[51]See *Statement of Uncontested Facts* (Paragraph 148) at 30–31. Most estimates of incidence of mental retardation indicate that about 50,000 mentally retarded children are excluded from any education in the Commonwealth today. See, e.g. D. Stedman and D. Sherwood, *Hypothetical Community, Average Incidence of Mental Retardation Based on 1965 Census Figures in Four Populations 100,000 People* (1967). Although Section 13–1372 of the School Code requires that *every* district superintendent report to the proper intermediate unit on every exceptional child in his district, no such census is now attempted or completed. (See *Statement of Uncontested Facts*, paragraph 148 n. 1 at 31.) Consequently, experts can only guess how many children are presently excluded.

[52]N.T. at 65–66 (Hearing of December 15, 1971).

retarded persons at Dallas State Correction Institution, 3,462 at State
mental hospitals and 104 in Youth Development Centers. And:

Fewer than two percent of the residents of Pennsylvania's state schools
leave the rolls each year; and half of those by death, rather than by
discharge. A discharge rate of less than one percent has two implications:
First, that beds are not opening up for persons in the community who need
them; and second, that the state institutions continue to provide a program
that barely rises above purely custodial care, if it rises at all.[53]

Finally, the Report concludes:

Nowhere is there a suitable commonwealth-supported local program for
children of school age who are adjudged uneducable and untrainable by the
public schools. Their normal fate is a waiting list for a state school and
hospital, at which services do not conform to the spirit of the school code.[54]

With these facts in mind, we turn to plaintiffs' equal protection
argument. Plaintiffs do not challenge the separation of special
classes for retarded children from regular classes or the proper
assignment of retarded children to special classes. Rather plaintiffs
question whether the state, having undertaken to provide public
education to some children (perhaps all children) may deny it to
plaintiffs entirely. We are satisfied that the evidence raises serious
doubts (and hence a colorable claim) as to the existence of a rational
basis for such exclusions. See, e.g., *Brown v. Board of Education*,
349 U.S. 294 (1955).

One further jurisdictional matter remains. Plaintiffs' complaint
contains two pendent state law claims which the Consent Agreement and our Injunction encompass. We find that, to the extent these
claims involve distinct non-federal claims,[55] this Court has jurisdiction over them because "[t]he state and federal claims . . . derive
from a common nucleus of operative fact" and they are such that "[a
plaintiff] would ordinarily be expected to try them all in one judicial
proceeding." *United Mine Workers v. Gibbs*, 383 U.S. 715, 725
(1966). Compare *Hurn v. Oursler*, 289 U.S. 238 (1933). On the other
hand, to the extent that these claims emanate from unconstitutional
results obtained by the improper use of statutes which themselves

[53] *1965 Pennsylvania Mental Retardation Plan* at 39.

[54] *Id.* at 93.

[55] In this case, Sections 1326 and 1330 are challenged primarily under State law while
Sections 1375 and 1304 are attacked separately under the federal Constitution.

are not unconstitutional, plaintiffs, of course, have made out a federal claim. See 42 U.S.C. § 1983.[56]

II. Abstention

Lancaster-Lebanon vigorously contends that we should abstain, and stay our hand until the Pennsylvania courts decide whether the Constitution and laws of Pennsylvania already afford plaintiffs the rights they seek to establish in this federal suit. For the reasons discussed below, which are somewhat unique in the history of the doctrine of abstention, we decline to abstain in this case.

We begin with the cardinal, yet often forgotten proposition that abstention is an equitable, not a jurisdictional doctrine. See, e.g., *Railroad Comm'n. v. Pullman Co.*, 312 U.S. 496 (1941). Hence, sound discretion within the confines of judicial precedent controls our decision.

Preliminarily, we must once again consider whether Lancaster-Lebanon can even raise this doctrine at a hearing on the proposed settlement of a class action. As previously indicated, such hearings are traditionally limited to the issues of the fairness of the proposed settlement or other matters expressly involving Rule 23. And an opportunity to object is extended primarily so that those who appear might offer the court, which acts as a guardian to absent class members, advice on the worth of the settlement agreement. Moreover, since the theoretical basis of class actions assumes that all members are bound by the legal strategies of those representing the class (provided such representation is adequate), we think that Rule 23 precludes Lancaster-Lebanon from raising the issue of abstention. Nevertheless, because abstention involves important considerations of federal-state relations, we have decided to entertain it in this case.

The doctrine of abstention applies in narrow circumstances where a decision concerning a question of state law might be adequate to dispose of the case or may change the precise nature of the constitutional questions presented, and the answer to the state question

---

[56]We also note that it remains within our discretion to adjudicate these state matters (and the question of unconstitutional results obtained under state statutes) *as a three-judge court* since other claims in this suit clearly demand such a court. See *Rosado v. Wyman*, 397 U.S. 397 (1970); *Florida Lime Growers v. Jacobson*, 362 U.S. 73 (1960); *Spencer v. Kugler*, _____ F.2d _____ (3rd Cir. 1972) (Aldisert, J). Consequently, we have not exceeded our jurisdiction by encompassing all of plaintiffs' claims within our Order and Injunction.

Some question may arise as to our jurisdiction to enjoin the defendants from denying plaintiffs tuition or tuition maintenance under Section 1376; homebound instruction under Section 1372(3), or pre-school education under Sec. 1371(1) since these matters were not expressly included in the pleadings. However, we believe that a compromise under Rule 23 may include related claims not actually pleaded in the action, and for this reason the power exists to enforce these three parts of the Consent Agreement. See *Winkelman v. General Motors*, 48 F. Supp. 490 (S.D.N.Y. 1942). In any case, with leave of court, plaintiffs could simply amend their complaint.

involves unclear state law. See *Askew v. Hargrave*, 401 U.S. 476 (1971); *Reetz v. Bazanich*, 397 U.S. 82 (1970): *Harman v. Forssenius*, 380 U.S. 528, 534 (1965); *Railroad Comm'n. of Texas v. Pullman Co.*, supra; *Gere v. Stanley*, supra. The rationale behind this rule is two-fold. First, by abstaining, the federal court avoids needless, or at least, premature constitutional adjudication. Secondly, it avoids needless friction in federal-state relations. This second consideration becomes particularly weighty where a matter of paramount interest to the state, requiring local expertise to resolve, is involved. See, e.g., *Railroad Comm'n. of Texas v. Pullman*, supra; *Bradford v. Sun Oil*, 319 U.S. 315 (1943).

Where there is no question of unclear state law, however, a federal court may *not* abstain merely because (1) state courts are as competent a forum to decide federal questions as are the federal courts, see *Wisconsin v. Constantineau*, supra; *Zwickler v. Koota*, 389 U.S. 241, 248 (1967); *Gere v. Stanley*, supra at 208–09; or (2) paramount state interests are challenged in the suit, see, *King-Smith v. Aaron*, _____F.2d _____n.3 (3rd Cir. 1972); *Garvein v. Rosenau*, _____F.2d _____ (6th Cir. 1972). With this view of abstention in mind, we turn to the facts of this case.

It is easiest to understand the abstention issue if we first assume that no Consent Agreement had been presented to the Court. In that event, plaintiffs' complaint would have divided neatly into two parts—due process (procedural) and equal protection (substantive).

As to the due process claim, the statutes challenged are clear; they simply make no provision for hearings for retarded children prior to exclusion from school or a change in educational assignment. Consequently, it would have been improper for us to abstain on this issue. See *Wisconsin v. Constantineau*, supra.

The equal protection claim, however, requires closer scrutiny. The statutes challenged under this Clause (1375 and 1304) as well as those challenged under pendent state law (1330 and 1326) are all unclear, and as yet, uninterpreted by Pennsylvania Courts.[57] Indeed, the very fact that the Attorney General of the Commonwealth was able to construe these statutes so as to eliminate the alleged equal protection claims dispels any doubt about whether the statutes are capable of saving interpretations. Moreover, Article III, Section 14 of the Pennsylvania Constitution[58] may already afford plaintiffs their requested relief.[59] Undoubtedly proper judicial procedure requires

---

[57]Sections 1375 (tuition and tuition maintenance), Section 1372(3) (homebound instruction) and Section 1371(1) (pre-school education) which the Consent Agreement encompasses are also unclear.

[58]See note 6, *supra*.

[59]Article III, Section 14 was adopted in 1967 and has not yet been adequately interpreted by Pennsylvania courts.

that a federal court allow the state courts to face these state law issues before allowing an attack on federal constitutional grounds in the federal court. Hence, assuming that no Consent Agreement was presented, we would have been faced with an unusual situation —divisible abstention—half of the case commanding abstention and the other half requiring a decision. Under these circumstances, primarily because of the distinctiveness of the two issues and the fact that the federal due process claim could not have been avoided on state grounds, it would have been sensible to abstain on the equal protection issue but decide the due process question.[60] Such a severance nicely satisfies both the demand that we accept jurisdiction where properly invoked and the requirement that we avoid needless constitutional decisions on local matters.

Since, in any event, we would not have abstained on the due process claim, the narrow issue before us is whether, given the existence of a final Consent Agreement, we ought now to abstain on the issue of equal protection.[61] Considering the present posture of this suit, we hold that judicial precedent as well as equitable principles dictate against such a disposition.

To recapitulate, the fact that a question of state law adequate to dispose of the case involves unclear state law does not in itself trigger abstention. Rather, the decision to abstain flows ultimately from the fact that the federal court's handling of unclear state law may cause a needless constitutional decision as well as undue friction between the state and federal systems. Consequently, regardless of any unclear state law, if it is possible for federal litigation to go forward without violating either of these underlying precepts, abstention must be regarded as inappropriate. In this case, by approving the Amended Consent Agreement and Stipulation we avoid treading upon either precept.

First, there is no risk of a needless or premature constitutional decision since the settlement itself eliminates the need to make *any* constitutional decisions at all concerning these unclear state statutes. Secondly, we find no risk of friction with the State of Pennsylvania in the administration of its local affairs since the Attorney General, Secretary of Education and Secretary of Welfare, the very officers who are responsible for administering the state's system of education, all affirmatively request that this court retain jurisdiction and *not* abstain.[62]

---

[60]We express no opinion on the proper disposition where the evidence on both claims is the same, and hence the issues are not easily separated.

[61]We point out that this issue differs from the issue discussed above, which was, what might have been done with this case if the defendants had pressed the abstention issue from the beginning or if no settlement effort had been undertaken.

[62]N.T. at 58–59 (Hearing of February 7th, 1972). See also *Corporation of Haverford College v. Reeher*, 329 F. Supp. 1196, 1201 (E. D. Pa. 1971) (Joseph S. Lord, III, C.J.).

Equitable considerations are equally strong against abstention. We have held a half dozen hearings over the last year. We have heard from international experts in the field of education of retarded children. We have heard from local experts on the administrative and legal problems. On the basis of their combined expertise, the Consent Agreements were formulated. Indeed, the Director of the Bureau of Special Education for the Commonwealth testified that he personally reviewed the October 7th Agreement "word by word, phrase by phrase."[63] And he worked through more than six drafts.[64] Likewise, the Commissioner of the Office of Mental Retardation, Department of Welfare, testified that he assigned one employee to work full time on the Agreement.[65] In short, the Consent was not drawn up by a remote federal court, rather it was prepared in large part by the most talented local experts in the Commonwealth, the defendants themselves. Certainly no state court could hope for more expertise in these matters than that supplied by the defendants in this case.

Furthermore, the plan which the Consent Agreement contemplates, which may make possible for many of the plaintiffs a life of dignity and meaning, is well on its way toward becoming a reality. The Masters have already expended much time and energy, and they have held several meetings in this Courthouse. Many school districts have begun the task of locating members of the plaintiff class. With all these wheels in motion, no useful purpose would be served by the court abstaining at this juncture.[66]

III. Fairness of the Settlement

The final matter for our consideration is whether to approve the settlement as fair and reasonable. In arriving at such a decision, we must consider its fairness to both the plaintiffs and the defendants since both groups are classes for which this Court assumes the role of guardian.

---

[63]N.T. at 29 (William Ohrtman) (Hearing of December 5, 1971).

[64]*Id.* at 28.

[65]*Id.* at 73 (Edward Goldman).

[66]Lancaster-Lebanon relies primarily upon *Reid v. Board of Education of N.Y. City*,———F.2d ———(2nd Cir. 1972) and, of course, *Reetz* and *Askew*. In *Reid* the Second Circuit affirmed a decision of the district court to abstain from deciding whether a delay of over two years between the testing and placement of brain-damaged children in public schools, with no educational services extended in the interim, violated the federal Constitution. But *Reid*, like so many other cases including *Reetz* and *Askew*, is distinguishable because the case before us (1) involves a settlement agreement which obviates the need to decide constitutional issues and (2) the Commonwealth has requested that we not abstain, thereby obviating the threat of federal-state irritation.

Additionally, we must dispose of the objections of the Pennsylvania Association of Private Schools for Exceptional Children (PAPSEC). Essentially, PAPSEC contends that the following paragraph is unjust *to retarded children* in private schools because it eliminates the requirement for a prior hearing.[67]

Whenever an additional facility or program within a School District or Intermediate Unit is submitted for approval by the Secretary of Education, then at the same time, a School District or Intermediate Unit, upon written notice to the parent or guardian, may in writing request approval of the Director of the Bureau of Special Education, acting as the Secretary's designee, for the transfer of particular children from private schools to the additional facility or program. Any district or unit so requesting shall submit documentation of the appropriateness of the new facility or program for the particular children proposed for transfer. The parents or guardians may submit any documentation to the contrary. If after appropriate investigation the Director of the Bureau certifies the new facility or program as appropriate for those children and approves their transfers, such certification and approval shall be in lieu of individual hearings as provided above in this paragraph. *Amended Consent Agreement,* Paragraph 29.

However, since PAPSEC is neither a party nor a member of either class, we must first decide whether it has standing to raise this issue.

To confer standing under the rules of *Flast v. Cohen,* 392 U.S. 83, 102 (1968), a party must not only establish a personal stake and interest in the outcome, it must also show "a logical nexus between the status [it asserts] and the claim sought to be adjudicated." In this case PAPSEC members no doubt have a genuine financial stake in the outcome since the Consent Agreement (particularly paragraph 29) may well tend to curtail the expansion of private schools for retarded children. However, they raise no issues relating to the welfare of private schools under the settlement. Rather PAPSEC seeks only to advance the interests and welfare of retarded children. It is not clear whether PAPSEC may do this under the doctrine of *Flast v. Cohen.* Compare *Pierce v. Society of Sisters,* 268 U.S. 510 (1925) where the Society of Sisters alleged both a denial of their constitutional rights by a state statute which outlawed private schools as well as a denial of the constitutional rights of their patrons. But we need not decide this issue because, even if we were to consider the interests of retarded children under this paragraph of the Consent, we are convinced that it is fair to them. In this instance, certification by the Director of the Bureau of Education, the opportunity of parents to participate in determining the facility's

[67]N.T. at 3–6 (Hearing of February 7, 1972).

appropriateness and automatic re-evaluation every two years are sufficient safeguards against an erroneous assignment.

Next, we consider the defendants, particularly the local districts and intermediate units which comprise the vast bulk of this class. When the objectors entered this case, they expressed alarm at the possible burdens, both administrative and financial, which the due process Stipulation and the Consent Agreement would impose. Subsequent changes in the due process Stipulation, however, eliminated most of the administrative burden, and that allayed the fears of all but the Lancaster-Lebanon Unit.

Lancaster-Lebanon continues to object to the basic concept of a prior due process hearing and asserts that injury flows to the school districts because under the Stipulation they will be unable to remove a disruptive retarded child from regular classes immediately. But this danger is more imagined than real. Dr. Sherr, Lancaster-Lebanon's own witness testified that the problem would arise, if at all, only with respect to severely retarded children. As to that group identification is rather easy; and an early identification, as required by state law, will permit a hearing and decision (if there is a dispute) well before the school year begins.[68] In any case, the Amended Stipulation on hearings provides that in "extraordinary circumstances" the Director of the Bureau of Special Education may authorize tentative assignment to precede the hearing.[69]

Financially, the burden of implementing this settlement falls primarily upon the Commonwealth, not the local districts or intermediate units. Dr. Ohrtman testified that the excess instruction cost required to educate a retarded child will be paid for by the Commonwealth. For example, he stated that if it costs $1,000 to educate a normal child and $1,800 for a retarded child, the State will reimburse $800 to the local district.[70] Moreover, the Commonwealth will pay intermediate units, in advance, funds necessary to hire extra personnel such as secretaries and psychologists necessary to implement this settlement.[71] In short, we find that both the Stipulation and Consent Agreement are fair and reasonable to the defendants.

We have absolutely no hesitation about approving the Agreements as fair and reasonable to the plaintiffs. Approval means that plaintiff retarded children who heretofore had been excluded from a public program of education and training will no longer be so excluded

---

[68]N. T. at 62–68 (Hearing of November 12, 1971).

[69]*Amended Stipulation*, Paragraph 3 (v).

[70]N.T. at 21 (Hearing of December 15, 1971).

[71]*Id.* at 23.

after September 1, 1972. This is a noble and humanitarian end in which the Commonwealth of Pennsylvania has chosen to join. Today, with the following Order, this group of citizens will have new hope in their quest for a life of dignity and self-sufficiency.

Order and Injunction

AND NOW, this 5th day of May, 1972, it is ORDERED that the AMENDED STIPULATION and AMENDED CONSENT AGREE-MENT are APPROVED and ADOPTED as fair and reasonable to all members of both the plaintiff and defendant classes.

IT IS FURTHER ORDERED that the defendants; the Common-wealth of Pennsylvania, the Secretary of the Department of Educa-tion, the State Board of Education, the Secretary of the Department of Public Welfare, the named defendant school districts and intermedi-ate units and each of the school districts and intermediate units in the Commonwealth of Pennsylvania, their officers, employees, agents and successors are ENJOINED as follows:

(a) from applying Section 1304 of the Public School Code of 1949, 24 *Purd. Stat.* Sec. 1304, so as to postpone or in any way deny to any mentally retarded child access to a free public program of education and training;

(b) from applying Section 1326 or Section 1330(2) of the School Code of 1949, 24 *Purd. Stat.* Secs 13–1326 and 13–1330(2) so as to postpone, to terminate or in any way deny to any mentally retarded child access to a free program of education and training;

(c) from applying Section 1371(1) of the School Code of 1949, 24 *Purd. Stat.* Sec. 13–1371(1) so to deny to any mentally retarded child access to a free public program of education and training;

(d) from applying Section 1376 of the School Code of 1949, 24 *Purd. Stat.* Sec. 13–1376, so as to deny tuition or tuition and maintenance to any mentally retarded person except on the same terms as may be applied to other exceptional children, including brain damaged children generally;

(e) from denying homebound instruction under 1372(3) of the School Code of 1949, 24 *Purd. Stat.* Sec. 13–1372(3) to any mentally retarded child merely because no physical disability accompanies the retardation or because retardation is not a short-term disability.

(f) from applying Section 1375 of the School Code of 1949, 24 *Purd. Stat.* Sec. 13–1375, so as to deny to any mentally retarded child access to a free public program of education and training;

(g) to provide, as soon as possible but in no event later than September 1, 1972, to every retarded person between the ages of six and twenty-one years as of the date of this Order and thereafter, access to a free public program of education and training appropriate to his learning capacities;

(h) to provide, as soon as possible but in no event later than September 1, 1972, wherever defendants provide a pre-school program of education and training for children aged less than six years of age, access to a free public program of education and training appropriate to his learning capacities to every mentally retarded child of the same age;

(i) to provide notice and the opportunity for a hearing prior to a change in educational status of any child who is mentally retarded or thought to be mentally retarded;

(j) to re-evaluate the educational assignment of every mentally retarded child not less than every two years and upon such re-evaluation, to provide notice and the opportunity for a hearing.

Arlin M. Adams, Circuit Judge

Thomas A. Masterson, District Judge

Raymond J. Broderick, District Judge

References

Abeson, Alan (ed.). *A Continuing Summary of Pending and Completed Litigation Regarding the Education of Handicapped Children, #3.* Arlington, Virginia: Council for Exceptional Children, May 26, 1972.

Abeson, Alan. "Law Review—Movement and Momentum: Government and the Education of Handicapped Children." *Exceptional Children,* September 1972a, pp. 63–66.

Accreditation Council for Facilities for the Mentally Retarded. *Standards for Residential Facilities for the Mentally Retarded.* Chicago: Joint Commission on Accreditation of Hospitals, 1971.

Adams, Margaret. "Social Aspects of Medical Care for the Mentally Retarded." *New England Journal of Medicine,* March 23, 1972, pp. 635–638.

Adamson, Gary; and Van Etten, Glen. "Zero Reject Model Revisited: A Workable Alternative." *Exceptional Children,* May 1972, pp. 735–738.

Allen, Richard C. "Legal Rights of the Disabled and Disadvantaged." Washington, D.C.: U.S. Department of Health, Education, and Welfare, Social and Rehabilitation Service, 1969.

Allen, Richard C. "Legal Rights of the Institutionalized Retardate: Equal Justice for the Unequal." *Mental Retardation,* December 1969a, pp. 2–5.

Allen, Richard C.; Ferster, Elyce Zenoff; and Weihofen, Henry. *Mental Impairment and Legal Incompetency.* Englewood Cliffs, N.J.: Prentice-Hall, 1968.

American Association on Mental Deficiency. *Directory of Residential Facilities for the Mentally Retarded.* Washington, D.C., 1968.

Berger, Morroe. *Equality by Statute: The Revolution in Civil Rights.* Garden City, New York: Doubleday & Company, Revised Edition, 1967.

Blatt, Burton; and Kaplan, Fred. *Christmas in Purgatory: A Photographic Essay on Mental Retardation.* Boston: Allyn and Bacon, 1966.

Cameron, D.R. "Educating the Ineducable." *Déficience Mentale/Mental Retardation* (Canadian Association for the Mentally Retarded), July 1972, pp. 9–14.

Chandler, John T.; and Plakos, John. "Spanish-Speaking Pupils Classified as Educable Mentally Retarded." Sacramento: California State Department of Education, 1969.

Crosby, Kenneth G. "Standards for Educational Services in Residential Facilities for the Mentally Retarded." *Education and Training of the Mentally Retarded,* February 1972, pp. 3–7.

Dinkelspiel, Martin J. "Recent Legislative Acts for the Benefit of the Mentally Retarded." *Journal of the State Bar of California,* March-April 1969, pp. 219–227.

Doll, Eugene E. "A Historical Survey of Research and Management of Mental Retardation in the United States." In Trapp, E. Philip; and Himelstein, Philip. *Readings on the Exceptional Child.* New York: Appleton-Century-Crofts, 1962.

Douglass, Joseph H. "The Rights of the Retarded." President's Committee on Mental Retardation, 1972 (mimeographed).

Dybwad, Gunnar. *Challenges in Mental Retardation.* New York: Columbia University Press, 1964.

Ellis, Norman R. (ed.). *International Review of Research in Mental Retardation.* New York: Academic Press, Vols. 1–5, 1966–1971.

Exceptional Children, especially Summer 1970, pp. 709–716; September 1970, pp. 43–49; February 1971, pp. 421–433; May 1971, pp. 697–701; Summer 1971, pp. 745–749; September 1971, pp. 5–12; October 1971, pp. 181–187; March 1972, pp. 517–525, 527–535, 537–545, 553–564; May 1972, pp. 735–738, 745–749.

The Exceptional Parent, especially December 1971–January 1972 ("The Pennsylvania Court Orders," including interview with Joseph T. Weingold, pp. 8–12) and April-May 1972 ("Business as Usual," interview with Gunnar Dybwad, pp. 6–9).

Foucault, Michel. *Madness and Civilization: A History of Insanity in the Age of Reason.* New York: New American Library, 1971.

Friedman, Paul. "Mental Retardation and the Law: A Report on Status of Current Court Cases." Washington, D.C.: Office of Mental Retardation Coordination, U.S. Department of Health, Education, and Welfare, June 9, 1972.

Garrison, Mortimer, Jr.; and Hammill, Donald D. "Who Are the Retarded?" *Exceptional Children,* September 1971, pp. 13–20.

Goffman, Erving. *Stigma: Notes on the Management of Spoiled Identity.* Englewood Cliffs, N.J.: Prentice-Hall, 1963.

Goldberg, I. Ignacy, "Guide for Further Development of Special Education Programs at Teachers College, Columbia University." Ed.D. Project, Teachers College, Columbia University, 1952 (unpublished).

Goldberg, I. Ignacy. "Human Rights for the Mentally Retarded in the School System." *Mental Retardation,* December 1971, pp. 3–7.

Goldberg, I. Ignacy. "Toward a Systematic Approach to Educational Planning for the TMR." *Education and Training of the Mentally Retarded,* December 1971a, pp. 148–155.

Guarino, Robert; and Sage, Daniel D. "Support in the Private Sector: The Effects of One Legislative Provision." *Exceptional Children,* May 1972, pp. 745–749.

Gumpert, David. "Unequal Rights: Denial of Education to Abnormal Children Spurs Parent Protests." *Wall Street Journal,* March 27, 1972, p. 1.

Hall, Em. "The Politics of Special Education." Harvard Center for Law and Education, *Inequality in Education,* Numbers Three and Four, March 1970, pp. 17–22; and "Litigation Strategies: Mentally Retarded Musical Chairs," *ibid.,* pp. 22–25.

Harvard University Center for Law and Education. *Classification Materials.* Cambridge, Massachusetts, 1972.

Hunt, J. McVicker. "Black Genes—White Environment." *Trans-action,* June 1969, pp. 12–22.

Hurley, Rodger. *Poverty and Mental Retardation: A Causal Relationship.* New York: Random House, 1969.

Ianni, Francis A.J. "Alternatives for Community Education." *Perspectives on Education,* Teachers College, Columbia University, Winter-Spring 1972, pp. 16–23.

Jastak, Joseph F.; MacPhee, Halsey M.; and Whiteman, Martin. *Mental Retardation: Its Nature and Incidence.* University of Delaware, 1963.

Jones, Morris Val. *Special Education Programs Within the United States.* Springfield, Illinois: Charles C Thomas, 1968.

Katz, Alfred H. *Parents of the Handicapped.* Springfield, Illinois: Charles C Thomas, 1961.

Kay, Herma Hill; Farnham, Louise J.; Karren, Beth Davis; Knakal, Jeanne; and Diamond, Priscilla Myrick. "Legal Planning for the Mentally Retarded: The California Experience." *California Law Review,* March 1972, pp. 438–529.

Kirk, Samuel A. *Educating Exceptional Children.* Boston: Houghton Mifflin, Second Edition, 1972.

Koch, Richard; and Dobson, James C. *The Mentally Retarded Child and His Family.* New York: Brunner/Mazel, 1971.

Kugel, Robert B.; and Wolfensberger, Wolf (eds.). *Changing Patterns in Residential Services for the Mentally Retarded.* Washington, D.C.: President's Committee on Mental Retardation, 1969.

Kutner, Luis. "The Illusion of Due Process in Commitment Proceedings." *Northwestern University Law Review*, September-October 1962, pp. 383–399.

Lauer, Rachel M. "Position Paper on the Concepts of Normality and Deviation: Their Implications for Innovations in the Roles of School Psychologists." New York, 1967 (mimeographed).

Lilly, M. Stephen. "Special Education: A Teapot in a Tempest." *Exceptional Children*, September 1970, pp. 43–49.

Lilly, M. Stephen. "A Training Based Model for Special Education." *Exceptional Children*, Summer 1971, pp. 745–749.

Lippman, Leopold. *Attitudes Toward the Handicapped: A Comparison Between Europe and the United States.* Springfield, Illinois: Charles C Thomas, 1972.

Lippman, Leopold. "Community Organization: U.S.A.." In Wortis, Joseph (ed.), *Mental Retardation: An Annual Review, I.* New York: Grune & Stratton, 1970. Pp. 239–249.

Lubenow, Gerald C. "The Action Lawyers." *Saturday Review*, August 26, 1972, pp. 36–42.

Mayeda, Tadashi A. "Delivery of Services to Mentally Retarded Children & Adults in Five States." President's Committee on Mental Retardation, 1971.

Meenaghan, Thomas M.; and Mascari, Michael. "Consumer Choice, Consumer Control in Service Delivery." *Social Work*, October 1971, pp. 50–57.

Mental Retardation News, National Association for Retarded Children, January 1972, May 1972, October 1972.

National Association for Retarded Children. *Policy Statements on the Education of Mentally Retarded Children.* Arlington, Texas, 1971.

New York Times, January 8, 1971, October 9, 1971, and editorial October 13, 1971.

Payne, James E. "An Ombudsman for the Retarded?" *Mental Retardation,* October 1970, pp. 45–47.

Payne, James E. "Ombudsman Roles for Social Workers." *Social Work,* January 1972, pp. 94–100.

Pennsylvania Message, Pennsylvania Association for Retarded Children, Winter Issue, 1970–71, Special Summer Issue, 1971, June 1972.

President's Committee on Mental Retardation. "A Very Special Child." Washington, D.C., 1971b.

President's Committee on Mental Retardation. *MR 71: Entering the Era of Human Ecology.* Washington, D.C., 1972.

President's Committee on Mental Retardation. *PCMR Message,* November 1971, February 1972, May 1972, November 1972.

President's Committee on Mental Retardation. "Placement of Children in Special Classes for the Retarded: Background Position Papers." Washington, D.C. 1971a.

President's Committee on Mental Retardation and U.S. Office of Education Bureau of Education for the Handicapped. "The Six-Hour Retarded Child." Washington, D.C., 1970.

President's Panel on Mental Retardation. *A Proposed Program for National Action to Combat Mental Retardation.* Washington, D.C., 1962.

President's Panel on Mental Retardation. *Report of the Task Force on Law.* Washington, D.C., 1963.

Roos, Philip. "Misinterpreting Criticisms of the Medical Model." *Mental Retardation,* April 1971, pp. 22–24.

Roos, Philip. "Trends and Issues in Special Education for the Mentally Retarded." *Education and Training of the Mentally Retarded,* April 1970, pp. 51–61.

Ross, Hugh Alan. "Commitment of the Mentally Ill: Problems of Law and Policy." *Michigan Law Review,* Vol. 57, May 1959, pp. 945–1018.

Ross, Sterling L., Jr.; DeYoung, Henry G.; and Cohen, Julius S. "Confrontation: Special Education Placement and the Law." *Exceptional Children,* September 1971, pp. 5–12.

Rothman, David J. *The Discovery of the Asylum: Social Order and Disorder in the New Republic.* Boston: Little, Brown and Co., 1971.

Segal, Brian. "The Politicalization of Deviance." *Social Work,* July 1972, pp. 40–46.

Segal, Robert M. *Mental Retardation and Social Action.* Springfield, Illinois: Charles C Thomas, 1970.

Segal, S.S. *No Child Is Ineducable.* Oxford: Pergamon Press, 1967.

Seguin, Edward. *Idiocy: and Its Treatment by the Physiological Method.* New York: William Wood, 1866.

Stedman, Donald J. (ed.). "Current Issues in Mental Retardation." President's Committee on Mental Retardation, Washington, D.C., 1971.

Tannenbaum, Abraham J. *The Taxonomic Instruction Project.* Teachers College, Columbia University, 1970.

Trudeau, Elaine (ed.). *Digest of State and Federal Laws: Education of Handicapped Children.* Arlington, Virginia: Council for Exceptional Children, 1971.

Wallin, J.E. Wallace. *The Education of Handicapped Children.* Boston: Houghton Mifflin, 1924.

Wallin, J.E. Wallace. "Training of the Severely Retarded, Viewed in Historical Perspective." *Journal of General Psychology,* January 1966, pp. 107–127.

Weintraub, Frederick J.; Abeson, Alan R.; and Braddock, David L. *State Law & Education of Handicapped Children: Issues & Recommendations.* Arlington, Virginia: Council for Exceptional Children, 1971.

Wolfensberger, Wolf. "Will There Always Be an Institution? II. The Impact of New Service Models." *Mental Retardation,* December 1971, pp. 31–38.

Wottitz, Sandra. "Obtaining Financial Aid for the Education of Handicapped Children." New York: Legal Aid Society, 1972.